Taking Care of Behaviour

D1394022

Taking Care
of Behaviour

Practical Skills for Learning Support
and Teaching Assistants

Paul Dix

PEARSON
Longman

Harlow, England • London • New York • Boston • San Francisco • Toronto
Sydney • Tokyo • Singapore • Hong Kong • Seoul • Taipei • New Delhi
Cape Town • Madrid • Mexico City • Amsterdam • Munich • Paris • Milan

NORWICH CITY COLLEGE			
Stock No.	238784		
Class	371.1024 DIX		
Cat.	SSA	Proc	3WL

PEARSON EDUCATION LIMITED

Edinburgh Gate
Harlow CM20 2JE
United Kingdom
Tel: +44 (0)1279 623623
Fax: +44 (0)1279 431059
Website: www.pearsoned.co.uk

First edition published in Great Britain in 2009

© Paul Dix 2009

The right of Paul Dix to be identified as author of this work has been asserted
by him in accordance with the Copyright, Designs and Patents Act 1988.

ISBN: 978-1-4082-0374-3

British Library Cataloguing in Publication Data
A CIP catalogue record for this book can be obtained from the British Library

Library of Congress Cataloging in Publication Data
Dix, Paul.
    Taking care of behaviour : practical skills for learning support and teaching
assistants / Paul Dix.
        p. cm.
    Includes bibliographical references and index.
    ISBN 978-1-4082-0374-3 (alk. paper)
  1. Classroom management.   2. Behavior modification.   I. Title.
    LB3013.D585   2009
    371.39'3--dc22   2008026393

All rights reserved; no part of this publication may be reproduced, stored
in a retrieval system, or transmitted in any form or by any means, electronic,
mechanical, photocopying, recording, or otherwise without either the prior
written permission of the Publishers or a licence permitting restricted copying
in the United Kingdom issued by the Copyright Licensing Agency Ltd,
Saffron House, 6–10 Kirby Street, London EC1N 8TS. This book may not be
lent, resold, hired out or otherwise disposed of by way of trade in any form of
binding or cover other than that in which it is published, without the prior
consent of the Publishers.

10 9 8 7 6 5 4 3 2 1
11 10 09

Typeset in 9/13 pt Interstate Light by 73.
Printed by Ashford Colour Press Ltd., Gosport

The Publisher's policy is to use paper manufactured from sustainable forests.

Contents

About the author

Paul Dix trained at Homerton College, Cambridge and has worked in primary and secondary schools in London, Nuneaton and Birmingham. As an LSA, teacher and manager Paul has led thriving Creative Arts and Drama departments, year teams and whole staff training in behaviour management, assessment, PSHE, marketing and primary liaison. His work was highlighted by HMI and OFSTED as a key element of the work that led to turning round a school in 'Special Measures'.

Paul is Managing Director of Pivotal Education, a thriving teacher training company specialising in behaviour management. Pivotal has developed a unique and highly effective style of teacher training that delivers practical strategies through active and highly motivating training. Pivotal Behaviour Management Training translates theory into good practice, engaging institutions in sustainable training projects. Pivotal trains teachers, advisors, students, mentors and teaching assistants from early years to adult education. It works with schools in challenging circumstances, Education Action Zones, Excellence in Cities, LEAs, universities and government initiatives. Paul has co-written information packs and resources with LSAs from schools across Birmingham ('Thinkenstein') and is the author of a national mentoring training scheme for the government's 'New Deal Mentoring Service'. Paul is a regular columnist for *Teach Primary* magazine, *Teaching Expertise* and *Didactics World*. His first book, the *Pivotal Behaviour Management Handbook,* was published in April 2005. You can find more information about Paul's INSET training and courses on **www.pivotaleducation.com**

Preface

You don't need a personality transplant to learn and apply behaviour management strategies that work. Neither do you need to follow religiously the teachings of the latest 'guru' or sacrifice your teaching style for the latest system. *Taking Care of Behaviour* shows learning support/teaching assistants how to successfully manage behaviour while maintaining trust and positive relationships with students. It encourages you to create the most valuable framework for behaviour management; one that you have designed to meet your needs and those of your students. It does not advocate a particular 'system' or suggest that there are magic bullets for solving the increasingly complex issues you face every day. Use it as a self-training manual: develop your existing skills, build confidence in your capabilities, design your own resources, create your own realistic action plan, learn flexible strategies and understand why your own behaviour is so important.

🍎 Introduction

The role of the learning support (LSA) or teaching assistant is never consistent between individuals, institutions or classes. Some LSAs are treated as equals (in all but wages!) as part of the teaching team with similar rights and responsibilities for managing behaviour as the teacher. Many will lead small groups in the class, work with behaviour groups separately, lead extra curricular activities, supervise on school trips, divide their time between many individuals and at times take responsibility for supervised or unsupervised class teaching (particularly Higher Level Teaching Assistants). Others will struggle to find a voice in institutions and classrooms where their status is similar to the students. They will find themselves in classrooms where they have no control over decision making. 'My LSA can find out what we are doing when the students find out', reflects the arrogance of some teachers who don't want to work as a team or even give 5 minutes of their day to empower their colleagues.

This book makes no assumptions about the status of the LSA and takes into account the huge variety of circumstances they find themselves in. For some, the guidance on structuring rules, routines and rewards is relevant. For others there are practical suggestions for dealing with difficult teachers!

There is no hiding place as a learning support (LSA) or teaching assistant (TA). While some teachers choose not to engage their students beyond formal teaching the teaching assistant does not have this choice. Alongside formal teaching there is the to and fro of a less formal relationship. Drawing the lines for appropriate behaviour while building positive personal relationships with students is skilled work that demands flexibility, consistency and determination.

Finding yourself attached to one or two students for much of your working week can be a claustrophobic experience. As you gasp for air in the staffroom it can seem as though you have been landed with a new 'friend'. Perhaps a friend who wants to consume as much information about you as possible without giving anything away, or one who wants you to complete their work for them all day, or at worst one who does not even view you as an equal. How do you provide structure to a relationship that has none? How do you ensure that you take the lead in establishing a professional relationship when the student would prefer a personal one (or no relationship at all!)? How do you manage the most challenging behaviour with care and control?

When you see a good teaching assistant working with students, behaviour management seems effortless. Groups are often relaxed and good-humoured, the students are attentive and engaged in the learning, relationships are positive and there is mutual trust in the room. Students who are challenging elsewhere in the school seem to have undergone a miraculous transformation. Other staff accept that the teaching assistant has orderly classes but often attribute this to strength of personality, time in the school or physical presence in the room. Their behaviour management skills are rarely discussed because they are applied so discreetly that they are difficult to identify, let alone emulate.

No one wakes up one day with the gift of good behaviour management, and few find these 'soft skills' occurring naturally. What are the skills that effective teachers and LSAs have honed over time? What strategies are disguised by the fluency of their teaching? How do they get through an entire lesson sitting alongside Shaun without breaking out in a stress rash?

I spent long hours preparing schemes of work and lesson plans in anticipation of starting my first job. Having spent a year as a teaching assistant, then four years training, I thought I would easily be able to engage students in an exciting educational adventure with me at the helm. Lever-arch files in hand, stuffed with carefully prepared resources, I skipped to my first class ready to educate and inspire. I was confident, well prepared and eager to impress. The students, however, had their own agenda. They had been taught by supply teachers for the past two terms and had very different expectations of their new teacher. Within five minutes of starting the class, two had climbed out of the window, one was swinging on the curtains and the others could not be persuaded to interrupt their game of table football, which was by now reaching fever pitch. I called for help and a senior colleague arrived.

Silence and calm descended in an instant. The students listened intently to him, and with coats off and pens out, we were now ready to start the lesson. As he left I thanked him and turned to address the class who, sensing his departure, had returned to their former pursuits – a game of coin football waits for no man. Driving home after that first day I was close to tears. I resolved to seek out those who had the skills that I was lacking and learn them . . . quickly.

It was to those early mentors that I owe so much. Their classes were lovely places to be, positive, caring and full of good humour and focused learning. They showed me how to:

- communicate my expectations to the students explicitly
- gain a perspective on my emotional state
- empathise with students' individual needs
- remain consistent and fair
- manage confrontation and challenging conversations
- use praise and positive reinforcement instead of constant sanctions
- begin to build relationships with students who presented the full range of challenging behaviours.

Through them I learned that accepting support was not a sign of weakness but a necessary stage in my learning. It also served to demonstrate to the students that I was not alone but part of a strong team working to help them make better choices.

I wondered how long it would take for me to gain the respect that those mentors had. Two months after my arrival, the headteacher was relieved of his post and within a year the school was placed in Special Measures. It wasn't until the end of the first year that I began teaching some truly effective lessons and building productive relationships.

After four years of learning and additional training, I was leading the whole staff in implementing a new behaviour management policy and my entrance into a classroom now had a similar effect to the deputy head's on that first day. I had cracked it. It was time to move on to a new post at a larger inner-city school. I approached this new post brimming with confidence: after all I had behaviour management down to a fine art and had been there and bought the T-shirt years before.

Walking into my first class, full of the skills of an experienced teacher, I could not understand why the students were not listening, why silence had not descended and why the same panic my first ever lesson had elicited was rising inside me. A difficult day turned into a difficult week and a difficult first term. I could not see what had gone wrong. Slowly I realised that these students did not know my rules, my expectations and, most frustratingly, they didn't know that their teacher was one of the good ones. After sifting through my notes and reflections I returned to the strategies that had helped me in the past. Gradually I began to translate the skills I had learnt in the previous school to my new post. A valuable lesson was learnt: regardless of my presumed authority it was vital to concentrate on the basics, the strategies that I knew worked.

Acknowledgements

There are many people who have contributed to the development of the ideas and thoughts in the book. In particular Sue Smith, David Buckle, Simon Spencer, and the large number of Teachers and Learning Support Assistants who have been trained by the Pivotal team. Perhaps those who deserve most credit don't realise the impact of their contribution. To the young people who tested me to the full every day, those who said no, those who barked and those who beat me in battle I give my thanks and gratitude. In particular to David, Luqman and Kevin wherever you may be.

Paul Dix, 2008

PART 1

Managing Behaviour in the Classroom

Chapter 1

Things to Think About Before You Start

'Don't judge each day by the harvest you reap but by the seeds that you plant.'

Robert Louis Stevenson

Lesson planning

I know that the quality and appropriateness of the work given to students is not always within your control. Yet whilst this book can address the management of behaviour it does not seek to do so in isolation. (We will discuss how to manage teachers who miss the mark when differentiating work, in Chapter 12.) If you contribute to the planning of class teaching or plan work for small groups give yourself a fair chance to manage behaviour by differentiating carefully. Poor planning always makes behaviour management an uphill struggle. Be prepared to question the value of worksheets, cloze procedures (fill in the gaps), word searches, or copying from the book, board or screen; indeed any activity that is designed to occupy rather than engage. Students know when they are being 'occupied' and respond accordingly. This does nothing to enhance your relationship with them or help you to manage behaviour that may well already be a challenge.

If your additional planning and preparation of lessons is not immediately appreciated or students respond negatively to tasks/lessons that you have spent a great deal of time on, it is tempting to say, 'I spent hours on those discussion cards and you kick them round the room/rip them/eat them!' Don't give up. It takes time to change the expectations and learning habits that students have built up about what should happen in a lesson. In behaviour management you have to play the 'long game' and not expect immediate or even short-term gains.

Examine planning and resources carefully:

- Do they match your students' ability and interests?
- Do they interest or excite you?
- Are they relevant, stimulating, dynamic and differentiated?
- Do they challenge pupils to think in different ways?
- Have different learning styles and cultures been taken into account?
- Do sessions provide opportunities for individual, paired and group work?
- Is there space for autonomous and active learning?
- Are there opportunities for self-, peer and group assessment built in?

A quick self-audit of your current practice

	Always	Sometimes	Rarely	Never
I get cross and shout.	❑	❑	❑	❑
I worry that I may have been too harsh on a student.	❑	❑	❑	❑
I am consistent in managing behaviour.	❑	❑	❑	❑
I set clear expectations for my work with students.	❑	❑	❑	❑
I plan what I am going to say to students in conversations about behaviour.	❑	❑	❑	❑
I have clear boundaries for appropriate and productive relationships with students.	❑	❑	❑	❑
I find myself in unpleasant confrontations with students.	❑	❑	❑	❑
I focus on catching students doing the right thing.	❑	❑	❑	❑
I chase up students who miss deadlines and detentions.	❑	❑	❑	❑
I seek support and advice on dealing with students with challenging behaviour.	❑	❑	❑	❑

Why it is fun to be bad

'I have failed with this boy.'
Paul Dix's mathematics report at age 15

Many adults do not understand the pleasure of rule-breaking, the attraction of dangerous substances, the thrill of criminality or the challenge of taking on authority. As I am one of those who spent much of his school years indulging in those guilty pleasures perhaps I can shed some light.

There are lots of root causes why students misbehave or fight against authority but there is also challenging behaviour without logical explanation. Students who have come from homes where they are loved and cared for, students who are emotionally secure, able and attend every day, students without medical conditions or mental health problems, still behave inappropriately. Why? Because it is fun! It makes the day more interesting, enhances reputation, provides entertainment for everyone and is an opportunity to safely challenge adults and authority, pushing the boundaries of tolerance. Breaking the rules has tangible rewards. It brings praise from friends, excitement and danger, increases adrenalin, releases serotonin and so delivers physical and mental pleasure. While some colleagues, teachers, parents and large sections of the media consume their time with the search for reason and bemoan the failure of a generation, the vast majority of children who break the rules are doing do because it is fun, an adventure, an exploration of the boundaries of authority and a distraction from the monotony of some lessons.

Some students have good reason to be angry. Others are angry without cause. They use anger as a defence, to test your reaction or as an amusement. They are able to time their anger, switch it on and off and use it to effect maximum disruption to your working life. It is these students who can often be the most challenging.

I am not discussing this to make you throw in the towel but to encourage you to recognise the primary cause for inappropriate behaviour and begin to use this knowledge. Giving your energy to the search for logic and reason in disruptive behaviour may well be better spent searching for strategies to make it less fun and less rewarding for students who behave badly.

Making rule-breaking less fun

- ✔ Clearly define rules, rewards and sanctions and implement them without negative or disproportionate emotional reactions.

- ✔ When students are deliberately disrupting keep your response assertive, controlled and simple; disruption becomes less rewarding.

✔ Keep discussions about behaviour discreet and private whenever possible (one-to-one rather than in front of the peer or class group).

✔ Reflect on moments when the student is attempting to 'score points': be proactive by predicting these moments and manoeuvring around them.

✔ Don't complain about students publicly or do anything to advertise their status, enhance their reputation or cement their label as 'troublemakers'.

✔ Try not to reveal or display your 'emotional buttons': e.g. 'Any more of that and I am going to lose my temper', 'You are making me very angry, stop it now.'

✔ By using acknowledgement, praise and reward as the cornerstone of your practice you slowly make it more attractive to follow the rules.

Chapter 2

Managing Your Own Behaviour: Emotionally Secure Relationships

'I had a terrible education, I attended a school for emotionally disturbed teachers.'

Woody Allen

The principle

In order to manage the emotional behaviour of the students you work with you need to provide them with a strong model for appropriate emotional responses. This should be your primary focus as a 'role model' for your students. You need to demonstrate and be explicit about how you, as an example of a successful learner, deal with your own emotional responses and keep them in check. Students need to feel emotionally secure when they are working with you to enable them to use the rational part of their brains to deal with learning and behaviour challenges. A learning relationship that relies on emotional responses from the adult to manage behaviour is rarely consistent, predictable or productive.

The practice

Monitor and check your own behaviour in front of students. This is particularly important when getting to know a new group of students or an individual. They are watching for your reactions and may be testing to see when emotion takes the place of reason in your reactions: they want to know how to 'push your buttons'. Make a resolution not to shout or show anger as a part of your teaching style. There will be times when you need to raise your voice or shout to prevent a dangerous situation but if you want to model appropriate behaviour these should be genuine exceptions to the rule. When you shout at students (or anyone) or humiliate them in public the natural defence mechanisms takes over and the emotional brain hijacks the rational brain. The emotional 'trip switch', the amygdala, diverts the information on its way to the rational brain (prefrontal cortex). The heart pumps blood to the hands in preparation for fighting and blood to the legs to prepare them to run. That is why shouting 'ANSWER THE QUESTION!' rarely gets a positive response.

As adults we are aware of when our rational thought is hijacked by emotion. We all have the capacity to respond disproportionately or act rashly out of frustration with a student's behaviour. For some of us the emotional hijacking can last moments, for others hours. With students who have not learnt how to deal with the frustrations of learning this emotional response can last days and return weeks later if it is not resolved.

Model the behaviour that you want to see in your students. Arrive on time for lessons, prepared for and enthusiastic about learning. Try not to show negative emotional reactions when you are confronting undesirable behaviour but instead explain your frustration as calmly and clearly as possible. You do not need to do this immediately: e.g. 'When I walked away from our discussion about the mess on your table I did so because I was feeling cross. I gave myself time to think and work out what to say to you. We now need to have a polite conversation and find a solution to the problem.' Leave your purely emotional reactions for the privacy of home or with friends where you are not the role model.

Your students are trying to learn how to deal with their feelings; they need you to model explicitly how you deal with your own. Many of the students that you work with may have learned emotional reactions and outbursts from home that are not appropriate in school. I had a student who would persistently shout at me and other students during lessons for no apparent reason. It wasn't until I visited his home to talk to his parents about it that I realised it was not an aggressive response. There was no volume control in his family at all. With 10 of them living in a three-bedroom semi they had grown used to shouting, all of the time, regardless of the proximity of others. It took a long while for him to find an appropriate 'voice for the classroom' and understand my expectations. Don't challenge students' learned behaviour from home

<table><tr><td>

Look at me . . .

If you are working with a small group give students 'thinking time' to prepare their answers before any hands go up. You might like to consider reducing the use of 'hands up', which relies on a few quick thinkers and makes everyone else feel either inadequate or slow. Consider introducing more subtle rituals for attracting your attention. I often use: 'Look at me when you have the answer, look away while you are thinking.' Students enjoy the discreet nature of the communication and everyone gets the space to think.

</td></tr></table>

openly – by providing a strong model for appropriate behaviour you can send the right message without direct challenge: e.g. 'Now try a 5cm/indoor/private/muffled voice while I wait for the ringing in my ears to stop.'

Think carefully about how you create an environment and atmosphere where all students feel emotionally secure and have the time, opportunity and space to think and speak freely. Examine your most basic routines. When you finish explaining instructions for a student, add: 'Do you have any questions about this task? Please ask now if you don't understand as it may be because I haven't explained it properly and that is my fault.' It will encourage students who are still unsure about the task to ask questions without feeling they are at fault. If you simply ask for 'Any questions?' the presumption is often that there ought not to be. When students have difficulty answering a question in public try: 'Take a moment to calm down and work out what answer you are going to give. I don't mind if it doesn't come out right first time. You know I don't always say things clearly the first time.' Try to make them feel safe enough to take a risk with their answer. Students who are confident enough to take a risk by speaking thoughts are easier to work with. You can gauge their understanding of the subject and pinpoint areas that need revisiting. Students who will not speak out or take a risk often find literacy a challenge as they miss out a vital stepping stone in language acquisition – thought, to spoken word, to written word.

Share with your students some of the ways in which you control your emotional responses when you are learning. Let them see you count to 10, take deep breaths, pace the room, focus all your energy into relaxing your thumbs, recite a mantra or whatever method you use to keep your emotions in check. Talk to them about their learning, how they feel when they meet and attempt tasks that are challenging, unfamiliar or new. Then talk to them about your experience of learning. Demonstrate how you work around the frustration of not knowing the solution straight away. Post the lists on the wall or record them privately so the individual can see them during the activity. They will highlight some key terminology, serve as an *aide-mémoire* for managing emotional responses and demonstrate that learners of all ages have to find ways through the frustrations of learning.

It isn't always easy to check your emotional responses, and at times even the most experienced learning support assistant (LSA) may be unable to stay calm and controlled. If you fall off the wagon don't dwell on your mistake but deal with the fallout in an emotionally mature way. Explaining why you reacted as you did, and apologising for an extreme emotional reaction, will also be a positive model for the students. Sleep deprivation and tiredness are common catalysts for a loss of emotional control both for you and the students you work with. When you are feeling at your most vulnerable the assertive structures and language in Chapters 5 and 7 will allow you to fake assertive control until you regain your composure.

Parent on the shoulder

A teacher I worked with at Chalvedon School in Basildon gave me the clearest image for controlling the way that I speak to students: 'parent on the shoulder'. Imagining that every conversation that you have with a student is being overheard by the parent automatically changes your focus and can help you steer away from an emotional response back to a rational one.

By modelling and actively encouraging a calm and consistent approach to learning you will start to build relationships with your students that are free from tension and fear. You will afford students the security and space they need to access higher order thinking skills and control their own behaviour. Trust will begin to develop.

Watch out for . . .

✔ Making judgements about students because of their emotional reactions. Keep in mind that your students will be at very different stages in their development of emotional control. It is your responsibility to teach them appropriate and proportionate responses, helping them to understand why persistent displays of raw emotion can be so disruptive to their learning and the concentration of others.

✔ Expecting students to have instant empathy with your situation. Explaining that you have just come out of a meeting with angry parents, have an assignment to write by Thursday and have an OFSTED inspection next week means very little to a Year 4 student. It is more useful to explain that you are feeling snowed under by work and share with them how you plan your time when this happens.

Reflecting on practice

Warning: Labelling is damaging to you and your students

The inner or private voice that we all use for mapping our own understanding of the working world must be constructed with positive checkpoints. Labelling damages your relationship with the student, the student's self-perception and your ability to manage your own behaviour. It reinforces the student's negative view of the adult world, perpetuates undesirable cycles of behaviour and leaves your language littered with negatives. If in your head you are thinking, '9c are loonies, book-munching head-bangers, if Chantelle Adams is in today it's all over before I open my mouth, they're just losers, how do you teach the little devils?' then you are unlikely to reach that positive and assertive attitude that you will no doubt need for the next hour or two. Neither will such thoughts allow you to examine the strategic changes that need to be made rationally. If you catch yourself using negative labels in the staffroom there are some compelling reasons why you need to check your own behaviour.

The adult who tries being positive in the classroom only to broadcast negative stereo-types among colleagues will not be able to sustain the separation of attitudes for long. Staffrooms often reinforce unhelpful labels of students/classes/year groups too easily. The joking seems harmless enough at first and relieves the frustrations of a few. But there are dangers lurking. As the jokes are repeated they become common parlance. Groups of staff begin to refer to Year 3 as 'little buggers' and Year 11 set 5 as 'the benefit squad'. It begins to affect how you view individuals and your expectations of certain classes. It also begins to change how colleagues view you. Just as the students make judgements on your consistency, fairness and integrity so do your colleagues. What from the inside seems like harmless banter is open to a wide range of unenthusi-astic interpretations of your character. Wise professionals stay clear of public and even private verbal attacks on students. When they are confronted by negative labels and stereotypes they seek to challenge them with care, as they would in the classroom.

In a school where there is a high frequency of challenging behaviour the murmurings can too easily combine to become a strong voice. Unfortunately the voice does not look for intelligent solutions but is a defensive response designed to shield adults from responsibility: 'They are unteachable, what chance have we got with parents like that, what hope is there for these kids?' I have worked in situations where many staff were supremely confident in their ability, safe in the knowledge that they were not to blame for the appalling behaviour of their students. Their negativity crossed over into the classroom and students began to get the message that they were uncontrollable. A minority of students leapt on this opportunity to escalate the frequency of extreme behaviour and the balance of power was disturbed. It took months to re-establish the status quo and years to improve the behaviour of teachers and students.

→

As a LSA you have to play the cards that you are dealt. You can spend many years decrying the system or the ills of society, sticking labels on students to reinforce your own negative map but it won't help you manage the behaviour and learning of the students sitting next to you. Neither will it help you to sustain a positive and assertive voice in the classroom. Moreover students, and particularly those from struggling communities, deserve to work with adults who are unerringly positive, consistent and accountable for their actions, and who take responsibility for their management of behaviour.

Exercise

Find a quiet space to complete the task below. Give yourself 20 minutes to complete it, in silence and without a break.

Continue the passage below on a separate sheet of paper. The usual conventions of writing in English no longer apply. Justead use this writer's 'rules' for spelling, punctuation and grammar.

lorna said to me, 'You heard the story of why the dog wont show its eyes?'

I said, 'No, I never'.

She said, 'That's what happens with people on the way down form what they ben. The storys go'. She tol me the story then. This is it wrote down the same:

Why the Dog Wont Show Its Eyes

Iime back way way back befor people got cleavver they had the 1st knowing. They los it when they go the cleverness and now the cleverness is gone as wel.

Every thing has a shape and so does the nite only you cant see the shape of note nor you cant think it. If you put your self right you can know it. Not with knowing in your head but with the 1st knowing. Where the number creaper grows on the dead stoans and the groun is sour for 3 days digging the nite stil knows the shape of itself tho we don't. Some times the nite is the shape of a ear only it anint a ear we know the shape of. Lissening back for all the souns whatre gone from us. The hummering of the dead towns and the voyces befor the towns ben there. Befor the iron ben and fire ben only littl. Lissening for whats coming as wel.

Time back way way back 1 time it wer Ful of the . . .

The extract is reproduced from Russell Hoban's *Riddley Walker* (1982, Picador). This task was originally used by Malcolm Reed from Bristol University PGCE English Course.

After completing the task, fill in the chart with your personal reflections.

Personal reflections on the task

My emotional reactions to the task:

....

....

....

....

How I dealt with them:

....

....

....

....

Students who have a reading age lower than that of the resources that are provided have similar, if not stronger, emotional responses on a daily/hourly basis. A student who has a reading age more than two years lower than their age (not at all uncommon) will experience these frustrations throughout the school day and in most of their classes. Clearly no one can comfortably live with the constant challenges this creates. Students as adults find ways to protect themselves. They may become withdrawn and avoid work discreetly or, at the opposite end of the scale, engage in a range of more disruptive work avoidance techniques.

When I give the above task to adults on training courses the same reactions are displayed. Those who are highly literate and emotionally secure enter into the challenge with enthusiasm. Others seek support from people sitting close by, make paper aeroplanes with the sheet, repeatedly complain about the task and, in one memorable incident, become so angry and frustrated that they walk out of the training room. These reactions are typical of adults who are successful learners; university-educated, academically inclined, experienced professionals. You might like to use this as your 'reality checkpoint' when applying the strategies in this book and setting expectations for behaviour.

Key ideas summary

Key idea	Benefit for the LSA	Benefit for the students
Model the behaviour you expect from students.	You will develop a heightened perspective on your own behaviour as you focus on what your audience are seeing and hearing.	Students see clear models of appropriate behaviour for a learning space.
Explain to students what techniques you use to keep your emotional responses in check.	Being explicit about your own behaviour allows you to deconstruct reactions to emotional responses, examining cause and effect.	Students become aware of a variety of techniques to stop the emotional brain hijacking the rational brain and with support will develop their own techniques.
Design your learning environment and routines to provide emotional security for students.	There are less emotional flashpoints in your interactions; you create a calmer place to work.	Students who were previously reluctant to speak out find their own voices.
Create some checklists and charts that map how to deal with emotional outbursts or mounting frustration. Display them (on the desk or on the wall)* and use them with the students.	The display is an aide-mémoire for the LSA to use when frustrations begin to take over.	Students have a visual map of steps they can take to adjust and manage their own behaviour. Anger is defined and rationalised.

Plan it, write it, do it

Choose a strategy from this chapter to try out. Be realistic about your timescale for implementation and review. It takes at least 30 days to change a habit. Set the criteria by which you will measure the success of the strategy with precision.

Strategy	Resources	Start date	How I will monitor progress	Review date	Success criteria

There is a printable version of the Action Plan on the CD-ROM.

Chapter 3

Consistency and Certainty

'Fair and softly goes far.'

Miguel de Cervantes

The principle

Being consistent in dealing with the behaviour of your students means that they know what will happen if they choose to break the rules and equally what will happen if they choose to follow the rules. They view you as fair and predictable. When they come and work with you they know what to expect. Moreover they are certain that their behaviour has a direct effect on your responses. Your consistent response to appropriate and inappropriate behaviour creates a safe and predictable relationship in which to learn.

The practice

It is not easy to be consistent and this often requires a great deal of emotional control. Inconsistency, at best, results in students being wary of you and, at worst, leads to resentment and confrontation. Becoming agitated by the fifth student who interrupts you and snapping at them the moment they open their mouth relieves your tension briefly but sends confusing messages to the rest of the students. Inconsistency with students can also result in your weekends being peppered with regret and worry that you have misjudged a situation or student.

'Fairness' is a very important concept to students and persistent inconsistencies in your behaviour can damage relationships. It is hard work trying to remain consistent and fair all the time. Particularly when you are tired, overworked and dealing with the demands of students who don't stop to consider how you may be feeling.

> ### Dealing with inconsistency
>
> When you next reflect on an incident and decide that your actions were not consistent . . .
>
> - Meet the student when you both have time to talk.
> - Apologise for your inconsistency.
> - Explain that your goal is to be fair and consistent and you will be open about mistakes.
> - Thank the student for being patient with you.
> - Record the development of the relationship from this point onwards.

Make it clear to students that they should talk to you, in private, if they feel that they have been treated unfairly. Model an appropriate way of complaining for the students: be explicit with tone and language. Let them know when the best time to approach you would be: 'I will not discuss consequences during the lesson. If you want to discuss what happened then I am available. . . .' This will not stop all students complaining defensively when faced with consequences but you may be surprised at the students who do use the system and give you pause for thought. You may need carefully to show students how to accept an inconsistent action/sanction/comment without reacting immediately. Once they are sure that the complaints procedure works they will have more confidence in doing this. When students use the agreed system you should listen with care and see it as an opportunity to reflect on your own practice and build relationships. Be prepared for and encourage other students to support those who find it difficult to approach you directly on their own.

When you hear students talking about adults they discuss those who are consistent ('Don't mess her about, she always gets you') and those who are not ('I hate him, he shouted at me for nothing. I only asked a question'). They also recognise those adults who use praise more than sanctions ('She never shouts, she's really nice, I can just get on with my work'). They know when you are late to the lesson, unprepared, impatient or react with more emotion than thought. They are forming opinions about your consistency that are quickly set and hard to change. Students bring these attitudes and expectations to the lesson and begin the class with them. Lessons can feel like an uphill struggle when students expect to be treated unfairly or lack a consistent model.

The more they sense inconsistency the more they will be tempted to exploit it or defend against it and the classroom soon becomes an unstable place for learning.

Working with an inconsistent teacher: the radar

Many LSAs have the experience of working in a classroom where the lead teacher is inconsistent or has poor behaviour management skills. Working in this environment is not easy and negotiation with the teacher often difficult. In this case it is important that you establish your radar with the students who are sitting nearby. As students arrive, inform them that if they choose to sit close to your working area they will be within your radar; you will be catching them behaving well as well as managing any poor choices in behaviour. For younger children you might place a red 'RADAR' card on the desks in the area that you are using.

Explain to the students that in order for you to work properly you need them to follow the rules in this area of the classroom. These may be the same as the classroom rules or in classrooms that have no obvious rules you might establish your own. With your radar established you can maintain consistency without conflict with the class teacher. The fringe benefit is that as students realise that you are monitoring their behaviour carefully those who might wish to disrupt will choose to sit further away. Enforce your radar consistently and in time you will establish an oasis of calm in classrooms where a storm is raging.

In order for students to be clear about which consequences (positive and negative) follow certain actions you need to be consistent in your application of rewards and sanctions. Not all LSAs have the authority to issue higher level sanctions. You do, however, have a right and responsibility to manage low level disruption. The more consistent you are with applying these consequences, the more the students will become 'certain' that poor choices will result in sanctions and good choices in rewards. When discussing behaviour with students talk in terms of 'certainty': 'If you stay on task while you are working with me you can be certain that I will acknowledge it and give you praise and reward. If you choose to break the rules you can be certain that you will receive sanctions that I will enforce relentlessly.'

This can take some time, so you need to be dogged in your persistence. If you place a heavy focus on praise and rewards, you will have a better chance of success and the pace of change will be accelerated. Rely on sanctions and your behaviour management may be effective in the short term but you are storing up problems for the future. Without a balance between sanctions and praise/reward there is little motivation for students to make better choices: 'He is in detention with me every week but it doesn't seem to make any difference to his behaviour.'

I have worked in schools where the heavy focus on sanctions was not balanced with strategies for positive reinforcement, praise and reward. The sanctions were well supported by all levels of management and all staff were able to place students in detention whenever they felt behaviour was inappropriate. These detentions, held twice weekly, were vigorously supported by the management team and in the first few weeks of the new system there had been some measurable improvements in behaviour around the site. Intrigued by the effect of this punitive system I asked to look at the statistics for numbers of students in detention. On the week that I visited there were 236 students in detention out of a school of just under 1000. Everyone was delegating responsibility for following up incidents to the management team and although behaviour around the site had improved (perhaps due to their fear of the senior staff who held all the power) behaviour in classrooms was beginning to slide. The system was nearing collapse as students grew resentful of frequent, high-level sanctions and the deputy head struggled to keep up with all of those who owed multiple detentions. Balancing the system with graduated rewards and reconnecting everyone with their

Strategy Spotlight

Inconsistent or just differentiated

The fact that you use your professional judgement to positively reinforce the behaviour of some students more than others does not make you inconsistent. Some students need to hear your acknowledgement and verbal praise more often than others. Their short concentration span or low self-belief needs the gentle nudge of your encouragement to keep them on task. Others appreciate their good choices being recognised every now and then; many consistently receive very little acknowledgement and praise and can easily be forgotten with a heavy focus on particularly disruptive students. It would not be fair to heap material rewards on challenging students simply because they decide to follow the rules – your thanks and praise are sufficient.

You are differentiating your responses according to the needs of your students just as you differentiate your support. It is this differentiation that needs to be consistent for the individual. Focus on how you are being consistent with individual pupils even if your expectations for some are different in the short term.

With sanctions the situation is somewhat different and you need to be consistent in their application. It is important that students know that whenever they are working with you the same sanction applies using the same tariff. If they sense unfairness in this area it will damage your relationship with them. The only exception to this is when an agreement has been made with a particularly disruptive student and this will usually mean that the sanctions are harsher or applied with more rigour than those applying to the rest of the students you

→

are working with. You are unlikely to find the rest of the students complaining too much about this and they will already be aware that the student in question has different needs.

Be comfortable with differentiating strategies for individuals, or groups – this does not make you inconsistent.

responsibility to deliver graduated sanctions reduced the number of detentions significantly. It left the senior teachers with more time to prioritise those students who needed most additional support.

The support of colleagues

Your consistency is not only judged by the students but also by other staff. If you need to call on support from colleagues they need to be sure that you have followed the agreed procedures in spirit and in deed. When colleagues begin to regular hear feedback from students about your inconsistency their support naturally wavers. Dealing with minor indiscretions with high-level sanctions without warning is just 'crying wolf'; when you really need support it may not be there. Demonstrating your consistency to colleagues as well as students means that you can be trusted implicitly. When the time comes for you to rely on the vocal support of colleagues (and it will) and/or the support of the students you can be sure that it will arrive in force.

Watch out for . . .

✔ Judging yourself too harshly. We need to be consistent but we are not robots. There are days when we feel shaky, tired, irritated and like running for the nearest beach. Days when Colin's persistent refusal to work seems designed as a slow torture. Days when, despite our best efforts, we deliver an unfair consequence or act out of character. Don't beat yourself up over these occasional lapses.

✔ Worrying about giving out too many rewards and/or sanctions. At first your students will test the system. You may find yourself flooded by requests for rewards and/or spending a great deal of time giving and chasing up sanctions. Expect this stage in the introduction of new boundaries. When the students feel the system has been sufficiently tested and they can predict your responses accurately, things will level out. It is not unusual for groups of students to reach the most serious sanctions repeatedly in the first few weeks. Do not be put off by this, stay consistent and fair and students' choices will change.

Reflecting on practice

An apology works wonders

I remember being unfairly harsh on a Year 11 class who met me for the first time and were still grieving the loss of their previous teacher. It was a difficult lesson fuelled by emotional energy on both sides and I was inconsistent, unfair and angry. I left the lesson worried that I had blown it. I reflected that I could not ignore my own behaviour when I met them again and needed to address it with them.

I opened the following lesson by apologising for my behaviour and being as honest as I could about how I felt. They listened intently and without comment. The mood in the room eased and the lesson was calmer and more productive. The foundations for our relationship had been set. Later in the year the same students commented that they had been shocked by my willingness to apologise and that their worries about me had been diffused. If you reflect on your interactions and decide you have been inconsistent, find time to apologise to the student.

Exercise

List the most frequent positive and negative behaviour students exhibit when they are working with you:

Positive behaviour	Negative behaviour
....	....
....	....
....	....
....	....
....	....
....	....

Decide on the two or three rules that will operate when you are working one to one or with a small group. They should be ones that cover as many of the above examples of behaviour as possible. Don't be tempted to negotiate these rules with the students yet. You may want to when you have developed stronger relationships, but for now you are the professional, and you get to decide what the rules are.

The examples below may help:

- When someone is talking, listen, or 'one voice only'.
- Stay 'on task'.
- Bring the correct equipment to the lesson (including homework).
- Do not disturb others who are working.
- Stay in your working area.
- Follow instructions the first time.
- No swearing or offensive language.
- Keep your hands and feet to yourself.

Rules

1. ....
2. ....
3. ....

Use the CD-ROM to print out copies of your rules. You may decide to laminate them and have them on the desk while you are working with a student or pin them to the wall when withdrawing a small group from the main class.

I find frameworks for applying rules, rewards and sanctions that use graduated sanctions easier to work with. One alternative to this is a points system where all students begin with, say, 20 points. Different challenging behaviour attracts tariffs and staff remove points from the students' total. My experience with these models is that they can:

- encourage confrontation when applying sanctions as you are taking points away from the student – a focus on rewards can easily be lost;
- create an opportunity for a student to lose all of their 'chances' in one day;
- be more open to abuse when we lose our cool ('Right, that's another five points off').

With a graduated rewards and sanctions framework there are no points and everyone starts with a blank sheet every lesson. Students can clearly see what reward or sanction comes next and can make decisions accordingly.

If you have the flexibility to decide on the sanctions and rewards that you can use with the students you work with then the next sections will help you to structure this. Of course, in many schools the structures for this are already decided. Part of your negotiation with the lead teacher will be to ensure that your structure can be dove-tailed with the school system and with the systems in place in the classroom. There is more guidance on how to make agreements watertight and discourage students from playing off one adult with another in Chapter 12.

Decide what sanctions will appear on your graduated list for students who choose not to follow the rules. You should make it clear to students that if there is a serious incident, such as violent or dangerous behaviour or verbal abuse directed at you, you will not use warnings or other graduated sanctions but take immediate steps to call for support.

You can choose to have one or two verbal warnings before more serious sanctions are applied. Be explicit in your language when phrasing your rules. Avoid loaded phrases such as 'respect' or 'manners'. Use the 'popular sanctions' list (see later) for ideas. Each time a rule is broken the severity of the sanction should increase.

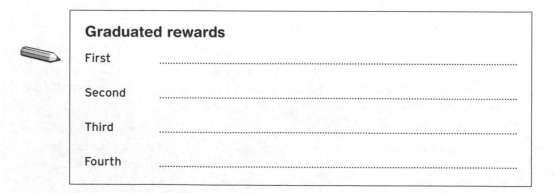

Graduated sanctions

First   *Verbal warning* ....

Second   ....

Third   ....

Fourth   ....

Now work out an appropriate scale of rewards. Again there is a list of ideas later to get you started. Rewards should be desirable, age-appropriate and easily organised. You may choose to have different rewards lists for different individuals/groups.

Graduated rewards

First   ....

Second   ....

Third   ....

Fourth   ....

Display this chart and explain it to the students. Use and keep to the rewards and sanctions you have listed. Don't deviate from the plan. When you catch a student following the rules, reward them; when you see them breaking the rules, warn them and then deliver sanctions. At the end of the first week review the chart and explain any changes to the students. Be prepared for students to challenge rules, rewards or sanctions that don't appear on the chart; they will help to keep your responses consistent.

Popular rewards

Private/discreet verbal praise

When you sincerely communicate to students how pleased you are with them it builds trust in the relationship and motivates them to sustain their efforts. It is the most important reward that you can give to your students (see Chapter 6).

Positive notes home

The most desirable reward for most students is positive communication with parents. Type up photocopy sheets of A5 or A6 with:

Dear Parent/Guardian, Just a quick note to say how pleased I am with ....'s work/behaviour/commitment in class today. If you would like to follow up with a reward at home it would be well deserved.

Keep a stack on your desk and use them as a higher order reward. Students will value these notes more than you might imagine. I had a Year 11 girl who still used one I gave her in Year 8 to wave at her parents when they questioned her school/social life balance *(see the CD-ROM for printable examples)*.

Post-it praise

Subtly sticking a Post-it note on the desk of a student who deserves praise communicates discreetly, without disturbing others, and in writing.

Positive phone call home

The most direct pathway you have to building a partnership with home is the positive phone call. If you don't know the parents well keep it quick and simple. Plan what you are going to say and how you are going to end it. I use, 'Hello, it's Mr Dix, Keenan's support teacher. I've got some good news, do you have a moment to talk?' and to end, 'I am sure you don't want to spend your evening on the phone to me, thank you for your time.'

Homework pass/extension

This is a token to allow the student permission not to do the homework or to hand it in late as appropriate.

Positive referral

Send a student, either during the lesson or at an appropriate time, to see a colleague for further acknowledgement and praise.

Merits/stickers/star charts/stamps

If your school does not already have a policy, or has one that is solely related to learning, you need to create a cumulative rewards system with tangible rewards at, say, 15, 50 and 100 points to support good choices in behaviour. Record merits in students' individual exercise books or homework diaries. Use an ink stamp or sheets of stickers or bits of paper with your signature and keep a record yourself. Don't assume that there is an upper age limit for such mechanisms. I have lost count of the number of times a gnarled Year 11 student has demanded 'the smiley elephant stamp'.

Group rewards

Post a sheet of A4 paper on the wall with a tally chart entitled 'Group Reward'. Any student can earn a group reward point and once earned they cannot be taken away. Once the group reaches 20/40/60 points they earn a collective reward. Differentiate the target total to keep your groups motivated. The group that struggles to begin the session will need a shorter-term target than the group you can easily get working. Make the rewards age-appropriate and desirable. For instance they might be able to listen to music while they work, work outside in the summer or have extended story time. You may choose to negotiate these rewards in time and ask them what they think appropriate rewards (that don't involve money!) might be.

'Leave first' token

Very useful if you have the students before break, lunch or at the end of the day.

Subject/class award certificate

Use as a higher-order reward and send a copy direct to the parents/guardians.

Popular sanctions

Warnings

One of the most frequent complaints from students who receive sanctions is that they didn't realise they had been given a warning. Find a way of clearly marking the moment that you give a warning: take the student aside, place a note on the desk or make a note in your planner. You can then refer the student to that moment later on.

Impositions

Students are given additional work to do at home that, when completed, is signed by their parent/guardian. Type up the instructions for the task and have five or six different sets photocopied so that you have them ready. Make a note at the bottom of the imposition explaining the consequence of not handing the work in before school the following day. The work should be linked to their work in class, be relevant, appropriate and differentiated, and take half an hour of the student's time. Do not give lines or repetitive tasks as these are completed with resentment rather than thought.

Lunchtime detention

I have never been keen on detention as a sanction unless I have an opportunity to discuss the students' choices with them. After-school detentions are difficult to enforce, cause complications with the timings of families and eat into students' life out of school. Lunchtime detentions are easier to enforce and have more impact (see Chapter 7). Keep the detention to 15 minutes; the length of detention will not determine whether the student chooses to repeat the behaviour. It is your conversation that has most chance of making an impact. Use the 15 minutes to reinforce and renegotiate expectations, perhaps finding an opportunity to build your professional relationship with the student.

A moment after class

Hold the student back after class very briefly to discuss their poor choices. You are showing them that you care about the choices they make when working for you. Most students do not like being held back as it means their friends will go on without them.

LSA's report

Keep a brief record of the student's behaviour in each lesson over an agreed period. Explain that when it is complete a copy will be sent to the class teacher, parents, deputy head, etc. At the end of each lesson read the comment to the student and ask them to co-sign the report. Be prepared to reward better choices as well as recording poor ones. Continue to apply your rules and rituals to students on report in the same way as others.

Time out

Give time outside the classroom, ideally supervised by another colleague, to allow the student a few minutes to calm down and rejoin the lesson. The language is important here. A 'time out' is less aggressive than being 'sent out' and echoes 'time out' in sport where players are given time to calm down away from the field of play.

Phone call home

An effective sanction but one that must be handled with care. Take advice from a senior colleague about the home situation and likely impact of the call: many parents use corporal punishment and this association may not be desirable. Think carefully about the time that you call and prepare what you are going to say and how you are going to leave the conversation. Expect your first call to be simply to organise a more convenient time to speak.

Moving a student (to sit elsewhere in the room)

It is important that when a student reaches this sanction it is delivered privately, preferably away from other students. If the interaction is too public you risk involving others and causing humiliation.

'Parking'

This is gentler terminology for moving the student out of the classroom to sit with or 'be parked' with another teacher who is teaching another class. Make prior arrangements with a colleague so you can send the student with their work. Give the student a prepared note or laminated card to take with them. Have a look at your school policy as it may determine what happens to students who have to be removed from the lesson.

Key ideas summary

Key idea	Benefit for the LSA	Benefit for the students
Apologise to students privately when you are inconsistent and unfair.	You are building positive relationships with your students. Your honest self-reflection is the mark of an effective professional.	They see you as fallible and human. Students are given a clear model for how to apologise for mistakes.
Have a complaints procedure for students who feel they have been treated unfairly.	Challenges to your decisions are not public and are brought at an appropriate time and place.	Students have a mechanism for complaining that is structured and mirrors those in working environments.
Design and display a list of graduated rewards and sanctions on the desk.	As well as providing a useful reminder while you are teaching the lists provide structure even when frustration begins to creep in.	Students know what will happen if they choose to break or follow the rules. They view you as predictable and fair.
Model consistent behaviour to your students by arriving on time, well prepared and with enthusiasm for learning.	Your modelling of appropriate behaviour and organisation for learning will positively influence your students. Your time-keeping and preparation give you a platform from which to monitor others.	Students have a clear model to use and interpret. They are enthused by your energy and given a clear example of appropriate self-discipline and personal organisation necessary for successful learning.
Blank sheet for every lesson.	Your expectation of a student in a single lesson is not coloured by previous incidents. All students have the chance to make good choices.	Students have the opportunity to change their behaviour. They know that you will always judge their behaviour fairly and in context. They can see that you do not hold a grudge.
Have a clear system for calling on support from colleagues when critical incidents occur.	There is a mechanism for dealing immediately with violent/abusive/dangerous behaviour.	Students know that there are some behaviours that require immediate referral and high-level sanctions.

Plan it, write it, do it

Choose a strategy from this chapter to try out. Be realistic about your timescale for implementation and review. It takes at least 30 days to change a habit. Set the criteria by which you will measure the success of the strategy with precision.

Strategy	Resources	Start date	How I will monitor progress	Review date	Success criteria

There is a printable version of the Action Plan on the CD-ROM.

Chapter 4

Learning Rituals, Habits and Routines

'This is the way we go to school,
go to school, go to school
this is the way we go to school
on a cold and frosty morning.'

Anon

The principle

Do not expect your students to guess the rules for each activity as your precise expectations will be different from those of other adults. Explain your expectations for each activity (e.g. sitting on the carpet and listening, working in groups, quiet individual study, going outside for break) so they are clear to everyone. Students can then choose to follow these rules and receive acknowledgement, praise/rewards, or not to follow them and receive (a) warning(s) followed by sanctions.

The practice

Do not assume that students know how to behave when they are working with you. Instead teach students the precise rules for each task. Good early years teaching is a strong model here as teachers of this age group spend a great deal of time initiating and negotiating learning and social rituals. From working in groups to moving furniture, from structuring peer assessment to asking for help, all students benefit from clear rituals that everyone understands how to use. Some of the rituals will be simple - like indicating that you need help by turning the pot on your desk upside down - and some more complex and structured - such as steps in negotiating group roles.

Break down each task into what is expected at each stage. Spend time teaching this. For more complex rituals involve students in creating attractive displays in the room on large chart paper, memorising the steps or chanting the ritual as a group. For simpler rituals use modelling and rehearsing, reinforcing appropriate use of the rituals with positive reinforcement. Phrase your rules positively, avoid use of 'do not' and 'no', avoid absolutes like 'silence' and value-loaded phrases such as 'polite' or 'respect'. At each stage describe the desired behaviour: e.g. 'When someone is speaking, listen' or 'Look at me.'

Marking the difference between learning time and social time

Establish a ritual to mark the end of social time with the student and the beginning of learning time. The clearer you can distinguish this change the more chance you have of getting the student quickly focused on work. If this ritual is modelled with enthusiasm then over time it will become predictable, consistently reassuring and safe for the student.

An example of a 'preparing for work' ritual between an LSA and a Year 5 pupil

- Greeting, smile, handshake.
- Three things that have gone well since we last met.
- Tell the student that learning time will start in 1 minute.
- Equipment out, coats and hats away.
- Stretch and shake.
- Prepare yourself for the task - equipment/resources.
- Mark the end of social time with a combination of: **words** - 'Right let's look at what we need to achieve today'; **actions** - taking your seats, opening your books; **physical cues** - adjusting the student's seating position, turning towards the front, looking at the speaker, 'eyes on me'.

→

- Agree the point at which formal learning time will finish: 'You have 20 minutes to finish this design, then we can take a 2 minute break.'

- Change your tone making it more businesslike, assertive and formal.

- Adjust your physical language making it more formal, with gentle urgency and keenness.

- When you break out and into learning time again repeat the ritual or a short version of it.

Teach the new rituals immediately before the task, giving examples and modelling your responses carefully. When the task is revisited it is vital that you run over the routine with the student. When the activity begins, focus on students who are following the learning ritual using praise and positive reinforcement to support their good choices: 'Thank you, this table, you have stopped your conversations, got your pens out and are listening. That is number two on our agreement, well done.'

When students choose to break the rules, give a clear, private, verbal warning: 'You have chosen not to follow the third part of our learning ritual. I am giving you a verbal warning. I need you to follow the agreed plan. I will come back in a while and will be looking to praise better choices.' If the rule break is repeated, apply sanctions. Indicate, perhaps by taking the student over to the display or referring to the list on the table, which rule has been kept/broken to reinforce the ritual. Introduce only one new ritual at a time and teach it until the students know it without being prompted and begin pleading, 'Alright, enough, we know the routine!!'

Investigate the existing rituals that the students understand and know from colleagues and use them when appropriate. For example, students who study Drama may have been taught advanced rituals for devising performances in groups. These rituals can be utilised in many subjects but particularly English, PSHE, History and RE.

Strategy spotlight

Nasty habits

Students that you work with will have their own rituals and learning habits that have developed over many years. You may find that these are detrimental to learning or are patterns of behaviour designed to divert attention away from learning. They will be easy to identify but difficult to intervene in quickly. Changing habits with a willing participant can take up to 30 days but for those

→

who don't see why they should change their behaviour it can take a good deal longer. It can help to map the habit or inappropriate ritual with the student so that they are aware of what they are doing. Plot sequential behaviours that you have observed on the map and encourage the student to contribute while reflecting on their motivation for the behaviours. Extensive research shows that as little as **5 per cent** of our behaviour is consciously self-directed. That means **95 per cent** of our behaviour flows from habitual actions or reactions to a fear, stress or demand.

As well as challenging inappropriate patterns of behaviour directly through your use of rewards and sanctions, consider providing or agreeing an alternative ritual. This two-pronged attack on the engrained pattern of behaviour must be supported by high levels of positive reinforcement and a consistent application of sanctions. Dogged persistence and patience in your demand for rituals to be adhered to will mean that rituals students initially fight against are gradually accepted.

Strategy spotlight

Countdown . . .

A good technique for getting the attention of a group of students is to use a 'countdown' from 5 or 10 to allow students the time to finish their conversations or work and listen to the next instruction. Explain to the class that you are using countdown to give them fair warning that they need to listen and that it is far more polite than calling for immediate silence. Embellish your countdown with clear instructions so that students know what is expected and be prepared to modify it for different groups:

Five, you should be finishing the sentence that you are writing.
Four, turn to look at the board.
Three, excellent, Marcus, a merit for being the first to give me your full attention.
Two, quickly back to your place.
One, all pens and pencils down now.
Half, all looking this way.
Zero, thank you.

→

Some students may join in the countdown with you at first, some will not be quiet by the time you get to zero, but persevere, use praise and the rewards techniques described in this book to reinforce its importance and it can become an extremely efficient tool for those times when you need everyone's attention.

You may already have a technique for getting everyone's attention, e.g. hands up. The countdown technique is more effective as it is time-related and does not rely on students seeing you.

Watch out for . . .

✔ Enthusiastically introducing rituals and then not referring to them again until sanctions need to be applied. Use the rituals to support your discussions with students. Point to and refer to them tirelessly until the students realise that you are not going to be diverted from them.

✔ Establishing too many new rituals too soon. Introduce new rituals gradually and over time. Allow one or two to become embedded in the learning before developing more advanced rituals. Too many new rituals too soon are confusing.

Reflecting on practice

'The wall of death'

As a young LSA covering a foundation class for PE, I was a little nervous. I had heard stories about the 'wall of death' but no one would explain what it meant and there was general merriment in the staffroom as they anticipated my adventure with the 'little people'. I had worked with this age group before but only within classrooms and then only in small groups on very structured tasks. Now there were 35 of them in a huge space and I knew nothing of their normal routines or expectations.

After a lengthy and not altogether calm or efficient 'getting changed' session, 'Just wear your pants then', etc. we walked towards the hall. I could feel the excitement building and they were keen to get inside. I slipped into my usual routine that I would use with Year 5 of leading them into the room and sitting in a circle in the centre. As I walked in, the class began running, en masse, round and round the hall. I reached for

➡

my whistle and giving a loud blast signalled them to stop. Unfortunately they did not recognise this as a signal to stop running and fall silent but returned the sound with whoops and shouts and by running even faster. I realised that I was encircled by the 'wall of death'. The class had clearly assumed that PE was just 'running about' and were having a great time.

I was saved only by a passing colleague (who may have been at the door for some time!) who got immediate results by calling 'freeze', which was a ritual that they knew. He quickly introduced an alligator swamp, lily pads and tunnels into the circuit and together we introduced more rituals cued by single words 'sleep' (for lying on the floor and resting), 'slow' (for slow motion) and used pieces of string on the floor to show spaces for small groups to work together. It taught me a great deal about behaviour and classroom management, ideas that I carried forward for older students.

Exercise

Create a ritual for 'Working with the LSA' and list five observable behaviours that you wish to see from all students, noting them in the chart below.

Learning ritual for working with the LSA

1. ....

2. ....

3. ....

4. ....

5. ....

Now display this routine on the desk as you sit down to work with the student.

Integrating latecomers into a group session can be very disruptive and time-consuming. Using a ritual for latecomers will not stop all students arriving late but it will help them to check their behaviour and help you to control their arrival so that it causes the least disturbance.

What do you want students who arrive late to do:

- Wait outside and knock?
- Take the seat nearest the door?
- See you at the end of the session?
- Wait for an opportunity to join in with the lesson?
- Go to their seat and get their equipment ready for the lesson?
- Speak to you immediately on arrival?
- Sign a late register?
- Walk in quietly without speaking to other students?

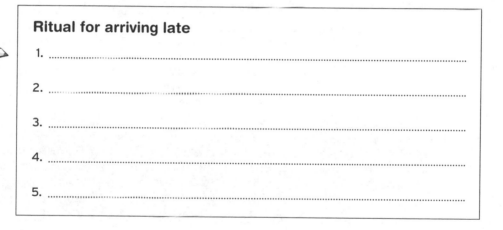

Ritual for arriving late

1. ....

2. ....

3. ....

4. ....

5. ....

Teach the students these rituals step by step, modelling the desired behaviours. Encourage their use with positive reinforcement and praise in the first instance and sanctions when necessary. When the students know them well, think about other rituals that you would like students to use and understand: moving around the room, leaving the room, group discussion, peer assessment.

The older your students are the more you will be able to negotiate and 'contract' routines. The younger the students, the more directed the rituals need to be.

Key ideas summary

Key idea	Benefit for the LSA	Benefit for the students
Use as your starting point the idea that all of your students need to know the explicit behaviours that you want to see.	The LSA can decide on the precise behaviours they want to see for each activity.	Students learn the specific desired behaviours that are expected; they are able to make informed choices about their behaviour.
Use language that is phrased positively when drafting your rituals.	There is an implicit expectation that all students will behave and respond positively.	Students begin to hear more positive language being used, their expectations are adjusted accordingly.
Acknowledge and positively reinforce students who choose to follow the ritual.	The focus and attention is on students who behave appropriately; inappropriate behaviour is not immediately rewarded by instant teacher attention.	Students learn that there are positive benefits to following the rituals; they are motivated by acknowledgement of their efforts and rewarded when appropriate.
Introduce one new ritual at a time.	The LSA takes sufficient time to ensure the ritual is embedded in classroom organisation and that all students understand how the system operates.	Students are given time to understand fully how the ritual operates and memorise the rules for each activity.
Investigate successful rituals that are employed in other classrooms; use and adapt them for your classroom.	We do not have to reinvent successful practice that students understand and can already work within. Students understand that there is a connection between staff and their expectations.	Students understand how and why you are using rituals. Their existing knowledge and understanding is used and not ignored.

Plan it, write it, do it

Choose a strategy from this chapter to try out. Be realistic about your timescale for implementation and review. It takes at least 30 days to change a habit. Set the criteria by which you will measure the success of the strategy with precision.

Strategy	Resources	Start date	How I will monitor progress	Review date	Success criteria

There is a printable version of the Action Plan on the CD-ROM.

Chapter 5

Language

'Language is a map through which humans construct their view of the world.'

James Britton, *Language and Learning*

The principle

Tell a child that he is 'naughty', 'stupid' or 'a troublemaker' and he will include it in his map to understanding the world. Tell him often enough and he will route everything through it. Through careful use of language you can help students to make better choices about their behaviour and understand the route to success in their learning. With students who have grown used to a negative view of their own ability the language you choose to use can help build self-esteem and interrupt negative patterns of behaviour.

The language you use can help to diffuse potential problems in the classroom, protect and enhance students' views of themselves and depersonalise challenges to their actions. The vocabulary that you use with the students is more controlled when it has been thought through and planned. Relying on improvisation is unreliable and inconsistent.

The practice

As a LSA you are often performing. You may not feel confident, assertive or positive on a Monday morning but you strive to give your students this impression. Perceived weaknesses in your use of language and tone of voice often lead to instructions being ignored or rejected immediately: '*Please* take your coat off, I'm too tired to deal with you today,' or, 'If you are not going to listen to me I cannot teach you.' Making careful choices in your use of language, and maintaining a consistent tone of voice and confident intonation means that you can communicate assertively even in a weakened emotional state. This takes some discipline on your part. You need to maintain an assertive performance even when you become weary of the constant inappropriate behaviours and your emotional brain tempts you into pleading with the students or throwing your hands up and slumping into your chair. Some of the key words and phrases suggested below can help you develop an assertive vocabulary and tone.

Assertive structures

'Choice' is an important concept in behaviour management. When students know the rules, rituals and expectations explicitly, then they can make a choice whether to follow them or not. All human beings make choices about their behaviour throughout the day. Teaching students that they can make better choices in their behaviour is an important aspect of your role. Using 'choice':

- allows you to attack the behaviour and not the student's character – *a person's behaviour is not their identity;*
- puts the responsibility for behaviour onto the student;
- encourages dialogue that is sharply focused on behaviour;
- draws attention on the student's own choices – separates them from the behaviour of others;
- depersonalises the interaction – 'This is not a personal attack, you have chosen not to follow the rules and I am applying the appropriate sanction' ('Don't shoot the messenger').

Discuss a student's 'poor choices' and 'good choices' in their behaviour: e.g. 'You made some poor choices in your behaviour today, particularly the standing on the chair and throwing your pen down. In tomorrow's lesson I need you to make better choices. I remember last week when you helped me to clear up, that was a good choice.' Help students to learn that all choices have consequences. Present 'closed' choices to students: 'You can continue listening to your Walkman and then have it confiscated, or you can put it away and carry on with your work. Make a good choice.'

If students immediately want to argue about sanctions or negotiate rewards explain that you will not discuss them in 'learning time' but can find time outside the lesson to do so. You may then have more time to provide more detailed questioning to help the student understand their own choices: e.g., 'What do you think the poor choices were that caught my attention?' and 'Which choices might have been better for you?'

Strategy spotlight

Closed requests

Many schools report the success of prefacing requests with 'Thank you':

'Thank you for putting your bag on the hook.'
or *'Thank you for dropping your gum in the bin'*.

The trust in the student that this statement implies, combined with the clarity of the expectation, often results in immediate action without protest. It is almost a closed request which leaves no 'hook' to hold onto and argue with.

A similar technique can be applied to requests for students to make deadlines or attend meetings that they would rather ignore: salespeople call it an 'assumed close'.

'When you come today arrive as close to 3.30 as you can so we can resolve this quickly and both get home in good time.'
'When you hand in your coursework next Monday, meet me by the staffroom so that I can store it securely.'

You are assuming and encouraging a positive response, making it awkward for the student to respond negatively.

Try out the following phrases and linguistic structures to turn a negative response into a positive one. The language has been adapted from sales techniques. You may just find that some work for your style and your students. Enjoy bypassing difficult arguments and skilfully turning a situation to your favour.

First 'No'

'I am certainly not expecting you to respond immediately . . .'
'All I am asking for the time being is . . .'
'Knowing what I know and being as close to the situation as I am I need to tell you that . . .'

Second 'No'

'I am not asking you to make a decision now'.
'Based on this conversation I believe what you are saying is . . .'
'Remember this is simply . . .'
'All I am asking for is 5 per cent of your trust and confidence, I will earn the other 95 per cent . . .' (Cheesy but it works!)

Third 'No'

'There is a very good reason that I have the persistence that I do . . .'
'Look what I stand to lose . . .'
'Give me your confidence in some small way now and I will . . .'
'I don't normally do this but . . .'
'I will promise you three things . . .'

As a final attempt at getting a positive response try:

'You don't make quick decisions and that is good, I don't make quick decisions either . . .'
'Listen, when I am in a situation like this . . .'

I am not suggesting that you change your classroom style into that of a used car salesman. Instead use the odd technique to sell successfully an unwelcome demand.

Many adults recognise that their pattern of behaviour is to be nice or compliant for far longer than they really want until they reach the point of no longer being able to hold it in; then they explode nastily and inappropriately all over students who happen to be around. This can leave students with the impression that there are only two states or behaviours adults can do – 'nice' or 'nasty'. The shade in between, which is where assertiveness lies, is unused and eventually lost from the repertoire of behaviour management strategies.

Assertiveness is not simply standing your ground, just saying 'No' and repeating your demand (the 'broken record' technique). Just as students have choices so you have the opportunity to choose your behaviour. You have many options as to how you respond to inappropriate behaviour, all of which can be assertive actions. You might choose to record it and address it at a more appropriate time, ignore it (for the moment), confront it, walk away and consider your response, etc. Assertiveness is knowing that you can control your own behaviour and making considered appropriate choices in your response to students. Don't be afraid of saying 'No' and saying it with impact when it is appropriate. Be careful not to overuse it as it will soon lose its power and negatively impact on your relationships with students.

Examples of assertive terminology

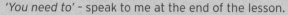

'You need to' – speak to me at the end of the lesson.

'I need to see you' – following the ritual.

'I expect' – a focused 10 minutes of work to end the lesson.

'I know you will' – look at the learning ritual before starting this task.

'Thank you for' – picking the wrapper up.

'I have heard what you said, now you must' – refocus your intelligence on the work.

'Let's . . .' – do this together.

'We can' – all succeed in this task now we know how to get over the tricky bits.

Making a deal

Everyone likes the thought of making a deal. The response to 'Do you want to make a deal?' is almost always positive. Without defining the terms of the deal students are willing to agree to it as it appears you are offering a compromise. In reality you may not be.

'OK, do you want to make a deal here?'
'OK'.
'Right, here it is, and this one is a special, time-limited offer. So you spend the next 10 minutes sketching that design without kicking Shaun and I will help you draft the paragraph of writing that goes with it. Look, I will even time the 10 minutes myself. Great. Deal?'
'Deal.'

All students, but especially those who have had a string of support teachers or an unreliable/chaotic home life, need to hear that you 'care' about them, their work and behaviour. I often tell students that, 'I'm here for the long term, I care about your behaviour and am going to work with you to help you succeed.' When you apply a sanction it can be softened by explaining, 'I care about your success too much to allow poor choices to stop you learning.' Students may not respond to this immediately but the drip feed of this language over time begins to encourage positive, secure and productive relationships.

Whilst our choices in verbal language are important in many situations only a small part of any spoken communication is carried by the actual words. Your tone, other qualities of your voice and physical language will carry a message four or five times stronger. You can say all of the right things but unless you pay attention to what you are saying non-verbally they will have little impact.

When searching for an assertive tone it is useful to separate interactions between those that use a 'formal register' and an 'informal register'.

Your formal register will be used when delivering important instructions, when calling the register, establishing routines, dealing with confrontation and disagreement, and applying sanctions. If you are carefully considering your choice of verbal language yet are not being heard it is likely that this register needs more attention. The formal register has little room for negotiation, it is directive speech, businesslike and at times brisk. Students should notice when you move into this register. When you have been working with students for a while they may pick up on the change in tone almost immediately. Some of your more challenging students will not like the change in tone and may seek to reject any formality in your relationship. With such students changing your register can be an important signifier that although you are open, approachable and positive there is still a formal aspect to the relationship. You are friendly but not a friend.

For a formal register try:

✔ A controlled, respectful but flat voice.

✔ Keeping the pitch of your voice within a 'normal' range. High-pitched voices signal frustration, perhaps signalling a loss of control, while low-pitch ones may signal tiredness or lack of care.

✔ Lowering volume and softening tone as you repeat instructions.

✔ Breathing steadily but not audibly!

✔ Maintaining a regular and steady pace of speech.

Your informal register which you might use when discussing work individually or with a small group, delivering personal praise, talking about areas of shared interest or welcoming students to the classroom, is equally important but is a more natural state and doesn't need too much shaping. Your informal register should be audibly different from the formal; more relaxed, more interesting and varied in tone, pace and volume. It is the sort of register that you would use with friends and colleagues. Students value being spoken to in an informal register but not all the time. The balance between the two is critical. Colleagues that have the two registers firmly embedded with students are able to switch from focused work to moments of relaxation/calm/humour and back to hard work. They can choose when they will accept informality and when they must insist on formality. Their students' own language registers become more defined as the model is imitated. Your modelling of different styles of speech can help to extend the students' own range and understanding of how different contexts demand different registers.

From the moment you enter the classroom your physical language is read (and misread), interpreted (and misinterpreted) and responded to by

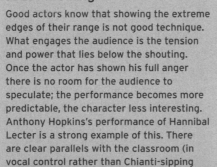

What actors can teach us about shouting

Good actors know that showing the extreme edges of their range is not good technique. What engages the audience is the tension and power that lies below the shouting. Once the actor has shown his full anger there is no room for the audience to speculate; the performance becomes more predictable, the character less interesting. Anthony Hopkins's performance of Hannibal Lecter is a strong example of this. There are clear parallels with the classroom (in vocal control rather than Chianti-sipping cannibalism!).

The adult who shows the limits of his range has nowhere to go next. LSAs who repeatedly scream and shout are often ignored. The 'audience' has become tired of the performance: it is expected, predictably irritating and uninteresting.

students. Being aware enough of your own body language to communicate consistently assertive messages is a very useful skill. It will take time to achieve. As a first step, check that you are modeling appropriate body language for a learning space.

At all costs avoid:

✘ Pointing at students with your finger, or at the door, 'Get out!' etc.

✘ Rolling your eyes.

✘ Turning your back on students who are talking to you.

✘ Standing or leaning over students as they work.

✘ Invading a student's personal space too quickly and without invitation.

✘ Demanding sustained eye contact (an aggressive act in many cultures).

✘ Using any form of aggressive touch.

✘ Dismissive hand gestures.

✘ Aggressive tensing of the facial muscles particularly eyebrows.

✘ Using your size to physically dominate an interaction.

✘ Fast, surprising or sudden movements.

Instead:

✔ Use your whole hand to gesticulate in preference to a pointy finger (or keep your hands down by your side).

✔ Show questioning and open faces.

✔ Step back from a difficult conversation to regroup.

✔ Adopt confident and deliberate movement around the classroom.

✔ Use a slow approach to a student's working space.

✔ Hold conversations at eye level with some eye contact.

✔ Maintain a relaxed stance, arms by your side, hands unclenched.

While it is relatively easy to plan to use certain linguistic frameworks, words, registers and body language it is more of a challenge to monitor effectiveness. In observed lessons ask a colleague to comment on your use of verbal and physical language. Give them a checklist of verbal and non verbal strategies that you are trying to employ and ask them to observe and feedback on:

● overused words and phrases;

● students' reactions and responses for changes in language;

● tone, volume, pace and pitch.

Watch out for . . .

✔ Slipping back to the terminology that you have always used when your work becomes stressful and your emotional brain takes over. Practise using new vocabulary and phrases as you are going to work so that they become a natural part of the language you are modelling.

✔ Sending mixed messages to students by contrasting verbal and physical language, e.g. smiling when applying sanctions or giving a reward without establishing gentle eye contact.

✔ Using open answer questions to tempt your students into negative responses, e.g. 'What am I going to do with you?'

I'm waiting.

What for exactly? A bus? A hip operation? The end of the world?

40? 374? 1.333?

How many more times do I have to tell you?

Why am I waiting for you?

Because you like waiting? Because you have nothing better to do? Because you are very dull?

Buy me an ice cream? Give up? Adopt me?

What am I going to do with you?

Reflecting on practice

Silence!

It may be terribly unfashionable but I like to teach students how to work in silence. For many students there is no silence at home or around school and once they experience silence it can be highly addictive.

There was rarely silence in classrooms at School X. Those teachers who could attain it did so by terror and the majority had given up trying some time ago. As a Key Stage 3 coordinator I instigated silent reading for Years 7, 8 and 9 tutor periods twice a week. There was general disbelief from students but I had a team of teachers and LSAs who were willing to give it high enough priority. We decided that it was essential that all the form tutors read at the same time and everyone modelled the behaviour they expected from the students. This was backed up with a 'learning ritual' for silent reading which reminded students of their individual responsibilities and a tightening of sanctions for those students who chose not to follow the rules. I supported staff by offering a referral system that would require persistent offenders to read with me and an opportunity for students who read in silence to take the books home. We were fortunate to be able to spend some money and hand-pick books appropriate for age and interest including graphic novels, fiction and non-fiction.

We worked hard for two weeks, coaching students, following up sanctions, modelling like crazy (to the amusement of students I would insist they held the book correctly to protect the spine – a formal physical language), rewarding students who followed the rules and making it clear to everyone that disturbing the class reading also meant disturbing the adults who were reading. After two weeks something changed. Students started enjoying the silence and the opportunity to read a book. They understood that there was no way of opting out and liked the fact that everyone, including the LSAs, were reading. Teachers and visitors passing by silent classrooms with 35 students reading were shocked and impressed. Whole areas of the school fell silent after lunch and it was not long before the scheme was extended to Years 10 and 11. The longer-term impact on the culture of reading in the school and community and the school results at SATs and GCSE was marked.

Students will remain silent if they know their compliance is time-limited, purposeful and planned. If you repeatedly and unexpectedly demand silence for long periods without explanation you are digging a LSA-sized hole to fall into. If you want to ask for quiet, teach the individual/group a ritual. Use the countdown technique explained in Chapter 4 or use the assertive instruction 'Eyes on me' or 'I need you to look at me and listen.' Explain why you need silence and for how long: 'I need you to stop what you are doing and get your eyes on me for one minute; what I am going to say will help everyone with this task.'

Exercise

Complete the exercise comparing the language that you have grown up with, the language you have used in the past and the language you could use now. Start introducing the new vocabulary this week, so that by the end of the week you have weeded out the vocabulary that is not supporting your students' behaviour. Think carefully about where the language that you have always used has come from – possibly your own teachers, parents or colleagues – and question it hard.

What did you say?

Incident – throwing a piece of paper across the room

What might your teachers have said to you?

'..'

What would you usually say to a student?

'..'

And now?

'..'

Incident – shouting out

What might your teachers have said to you?

'..'

What would you usually say to a student?

'..'

And now?

'..'

Incident – refusing to follow instructions

What might your teachers have said to you?

'..'

What would you usually say to a student?

'..'

And now?

'..'

Key ideas summary

Key idea	Benefit for the LSA	Benefit for the students
The verbal and physical language used in the classroom is the result of careful planning rather than repeated spontaneous improvisation.	You make conscious choices over the vocabulary and linguistic structures used. When you are under pressure your verbal and physical language remains consistent.	Verbal and physical responses are predictable. The classroom environment has less tension and is a safer place in which to learn.
The LSA's verbal and physical language is assertive.	The LSA is more likely to get their needs met and correct behaviour quickly and efficiently.	Students are in doubt about who is in control of the management of behaviour. They can easily understand your instructions and read your physical language.
Discuss behaviour in terms of 'choices', confronting the behaviour rather than attacking the student's character.	The LSA is able to 'deperson-alise' conversations about behaviour and reduce the likelihood of confrontation.	Students understand that they are responsible for the choices they make. They soon realise that the sanctions that result from inappropriate behaviour do not constitute a personal attack.
Clearly differentiate between formal and informal language, modelling its appropriate use.	The LSA is able to establish formal and informal rituals in the classroom.	Students learn from and imitate the model, understanding that different situations dictate different forms of language.
Model and define appropriate physical language for the classroom.	The LSA establishes clear expectations for movement, touch, personal space, etc.	Students feel safe and have a clear model of appropriate behaviour for the classroom.
Steer clear of stock phrases and clichés that have little impact on behaviour.	The LSA is encouraged to create language that is tailored to meet the needs of their students.	Students have less opportunity to undermine the adults publicly.

Plan it, write it, do it

Choose a strategy from this chapter to try out. Be realistic about your timescale for implementation and review. It takes at least 30 days to change a habit. Set the criteria by which you will measure the success of the strategy with precision.

Strategy	Resources	Start date	How I will monitor progress	Review date	Success criteria

There is a printable version of the Action Plan on the CD-ROM.

Chapter 6

Intelligent Use of Praise and Reward

'Knowing is not enough; we must apply. Willing is not enough; we must do.'

Johann Wolfgang von Goethe

The principle

Humans are motivated by acknowledgement of their work, praise and reward. In the classroom, praise is the most powerful tool you have for managing the behaviour of your students bar none. If you relentlessly positively reinforce the behaviour that you want and expect, students will respond by seeking your attention through fair means rather than foul.

Using praise is not a technique. Sincere praise and positive reinforcement are the essential foundations for a productive, professional relationship. Praise raises self-esteem, increases motivation and improves attitudes to adults, subjects and school in general.

The practice

The rewards that most students value are not material but the relational ones of friendliness, warmth, acceptance, recognition, encouragement and the good opinion of others. The reward that most children cite as the most desirable is positive feedback to their parents.

You need to acknowledge students who are following your instructions and rituals with a 'thank you' or non-verbal sign (thumbs up, nod of the head) coupled with eye contact. This is a positive reinforcement of their behaviour, good manners and an important step to creating a positive ethos in the relationship. I cannot imagine training adults without saying thank you; the same follows for students.

You need to be intelligent with your use of praise as it has differing effects on individuals. Not all humans want public praise; in fact many find it as distressing as public admonishment. Hold up the work from a student as an example to the rest of the class and a broad smile may open up on the face of one pupil, but for another it is humiliating, unwelcome and may discourage them from aiming for similar standards in the future.

Students appreciate praise when it is delivered discreetly, privately and fairly. They should know that your praise is sincere and deserved. They need praise that is individualised and you need to be prepared to deliver this using your own language and style. Repeating 'praise phrases' will not convince anyone that you truly appreciate their work and ability to stay within the rules. Most of the time you will be sitting next to the students at the desk but if you are moving around the classroom get down to a student's eye level by crouching next to their working table. Right down, not leaning over other students, but so your physical status is diminished. Try positioning yourself so the student has to look down to you: it has a very calming effect on the interaction. Tell the student what you are praising and why and use physical and verbal language that reinforces the positive message.

Don't reserve your acknowledgement and praise for only the best-behaved students. Praise those students who quietly get on with their work, those who find progress difficult and those whose concentration drifts. Differentiate your praise; the student who struggles with written work yet completes the opening paragraph may deserve equal praise to the literate student presenting a finished story. Change your own perspective to 'catch someone doing the right thing'. The accomplished Year 1 teacher who brings their class to order by focusing on the students who are following the rules is a strong example here: 'Just look at Samuel, he is sitting up straight with his table tidy ready to leave for lunch. Well done, Samuel, you can go first.' The same technique can be as effective with Year 6, 9 or even 12 students. The language, tone and attitude must be age-appropriate, but with 16-year-olds: 'Great, you have your equipment ready and are well prepared, thank you,' has a similar effect.

Use positive reinforcement and acknowledgement to draw other students back on task without drawing attention to them. The 'off task' student may well be drawn back to work by your attention to the hard work of their neighbour. It is a gentler and less intrusive first step to sending the message, but not confronting the behaviour immediately.

Praise students as they are leaving the room, particularly those who may have been overlooked as you spent most of your time stopping Trevor from sleeping under the table: 'Thank you for your hard work today, Ayesha, you have really impressed me with your concentration.'

Intelligent use of praise

'Wallpapering' your classroom/table/area with praise and positive reinforcement is important. Being passionate about your work, motivated and energetic is certainly infectious but those who succeed with the 'hard to reach' know that there is more to praise than simply saying lovely things.

In your next lesson make a mental note of how you are using praise and see if you can get a balance between the five definitions below.

1. **Wallpaper praise** – praise that makes the classroom feel good, 'great, lovely, marvellous, splendid. . . .' There is nothing wrong with this type of praise but it can be used so often that it stops making an impression on individuals. Just as the shouty adult can easily be ignored so students who are constantly told that everything is 'fantastic' can miss praise that is directed at them.

2. **Personal praise** – praise that is aimed at the student's personality: 'You are brilliant, you are intelligent, you are really doing well. . . .' We might assume that personal praise is automatically effective in building the self-esteem of the individual. Personal praise works when you have established trust with the student and when, particularly with older students, they value your opinion. If you always rely on personal praise then the link between behaviour and identity is reinforced. Students learn to seek your approval for what they do rather than examine their work/choices and find the value in it for themselves.

3. **Directed praise** – praise that reinforces good choices in behaviour: 'Well done for following the rule, thank you for respecting the "one voice" routine. . . .' This is essential for teaching new rules and rituals for learning. Once students understand the boundaries 'directed praise' can become redundant: 'The way you have sat down, got your equipment out and drawn a nice straight line for the margin is excellent,' 'Err thanks, but I am in Year 11, top set and predicted an A grade.'

4. **Reflective praise** – praise that encourages positive self-reflection: 'You must feel good about the accuracy of this work.' Reflective praise encourages the student to examine the intrinsic value of their work/choices. Instead of relying on your approval they learn to approve work for themselves. Reflective praise encourages students to value their work and value their skills in creating it.

5. **Contextual praise** – praise that places the achievement in a wider context: 'That work is a GCSE grade C and you are in Year 8. Can I use it for the display?' Contextual praise allows comparisons with the world outside the one-to-one, small group, classroom and school situations. It can be highly motivating for students and gives them a sense that their achievement might have significance for a wider audience, raising expectations for future work.

For 'hard to reach' students who have particularly low self-esteem and a negative view of their own potential it is reflective and contextual praise that attacks this most effectively. Take a few moments to include some reflective and contextual praise for your trickiest students when you are marking their work. When you give personal feedback try to draw out from the student a recognition of their own success: 'Tell me why you think I am about to give you this sticker' or 'Why do you think I would like this on display?'

Strategy spotlight

Too much praise?

There is much debate about the amount of verbal praise that is appropriate to use with students. Adults are often concerned that if they use praise too much it will become devalued and they risk highlighting efforts that they see as being 'normal'. There is also a worry that some students will miss out on the praise so it is better kept for special occasions. Their caution often hides a discomfort with using praise and positive reinforcement as their default teaching style. I think there is some fear lurking also; perhaps the fear of appearing soft, too open, even weak. Yet for the students praise is very welcome. They view you as assertive, interested in their work and at worst a little over-enthusiastic. In 18 years of working in schools I have never heard a student complain that a teacher praises too much. However I often hear concerns that teachers ignore the efforts of students who work hard throughout each lesson. I believe that fears about using too much praise are misplaced in a culture that is prone to identify failure rather than success.

Adults who succeed with students who present high-level challenging behaviours will tell you that they use high levels of praise and positive reinforcement. It is not that they think these children deserve more praise than others. It is because quite simply they know that it works. They are not worried about overusing praise as they know that it continues to have an impact and is a far better behaviour management tool than sanctions. Students with low self-esteem, poor emotional control and/or attention disorders need and appreciate intensive and regular positive feedback. For some the intensity of the praise acts as a counterbalance to many years of criticism and assumed failure.

Touch

There has been great debate in recent years about touch. I have always tried to help students understand that touch is a human response: not necessarily violent or sexual but encouraging, affirming and a part of human communication. For students that you have spent time getting to know and trust, a safe, affirming hand on the shoulder or upper arm is not going to be misunderstood. Obviously for students with whom you have not built a relationship or those who are uncomfortable with it, even safe touch may not be appropriate. In many secondary schools there is great fear about touch. I understand the reservations, the scare stories and the knee-jerk advice given on touch. But what are we teaching students if we work with them every day yet stop ourselves responding naturally? In early years or primary contexts there is no choice – just try comforting a distressed four-year-old without giving him a cuddle – in secondary and FE it would be difficult to teach PE, Drama, Dance, Music or Art without some human contact. Before we distance ourselves more from young people it is worth considering just how far down this road we are prepared to go and how it will directly affect the society we are building.

When you praise Charlene for staying on task throughout the lesson you are doing so because she needs to hear it not because you feel like giving it. Assuming that students don't need praise for doing what they 'should' be doing anyway is as dangerous as assuming that they know how to behave. How long will Charlene stay on task if her efforts are ignored? Multiply this by your group size and it is easy to see how the behaviour and work of students can change radically between teachers/LSAs who use praise and positive reinforcement and those that do not. Remember, not all students receive praise at home just as not all students receive praise at school. Your interaction may not be memorable in your day but it may well be in hers.

Of course, as we have already seen, your praise must be age-appropriate, personal, sincere and with language and style that you are comfortable using. But don't worry too much about overusing it: it can do no one any harm.

Watch out for . . .

✔ Using all of your positive energy on the first day. Being positive and delivering praise consistently and fairly throughout your working day can be exhausting. Praise is hard work at first, especially at the end of a long day with a challenging group, but it pays dividends in the short, long and medium term.

✔ Taking away praise/rewards. If you give students sincere praise and perhaps a reward for their hard work it should not be revoked. If they make poor choices afterwards, give a verbal warning and then apply sanctions. There is no conflict in students receiving both.

✔ Praise and reward should not be used as a bribe but provided after the positive behaviour.

→

✔ Slipping back into negatives when praise doesn't work the first time. Your students need to be convinced that you are committed to a consistently positive environment. This cannot be achieved in one day and your positive responses will need to become part of your teaching style and not an afterthought.

✔ Passing over those students who work quietly and consistently throughout the lesson. They deserve and need your acknowledgement and praise. Without it they may choose to gain attention by less positive means. Stand by the door as the students leave and catch those students you may have missed in the lesson.

Reflecting on practice

Shaun's self-belief

At 14 Shaun was a highly disruptive student. He was often absent and when he did appear he was keen to confirm his low opinion of his own abilities and the inadequacies of his teachers. In my lessons he was a problem and would stand at the side and watch more often than taking part. There were rare flashes of limited enthusiasm that were not sustained. He demonstrated no more ability in Drama than in any other subject.

I felt for his mother touring the teachers at parents' evening and being traumatised at every table. All of Shaun's sins would be laid bare by teachers keen to vent their frustration at his continual disruption. By the time she reached my table at the end of the night she was resigned to listening to another litany of crimes and misdemeanours. I decided to concentrate on those moments when Shaun engaged in the lesson and left her feeling that all was not lost and that he had some opportunities in Drama.

The following day Shaun came to see me and thanked me for what I had said to his mother. He recognised the fact that it was not wholly deserved but was interested to know why I thought he had some ability and potential in the subject. I explained it to him carefully and he listened.

Shaun's head of year came to see me the following week to discuss Shaun's part-time timetable and was keen to include Drama within it. Shaun attended almost every lesson in two years, struggled with the coursework as he had poor literacy skills but engaged in practical work with real focus and enthusiasm. He attended theatre visits regularly and was blown away by mask work. Shaun only turned up for one examination at the end of Year 11 but he passed with a C grade and I will never forget the pride on his face when he came to collect his results.

The turning point of his self-belief came from that parents' evening.

Exercise

In the first week, use the tally chart to record the positive and negative comments that you give. Aim for a ratio of 5:1 positive to negative comments. Try to phrase a negative reaction in positive terms. For example, 'Thank you for sitting down so quickly, you will need the hand that is in Oliver's bag to write down the first key word,' as opposed to, 'Stop doing that, you are supposed to be listening to me, how many times have I told you. . . .' After the lesson note down any words or phrases that had a positive impact and those that you wish you hadn't said.

Positive comments	Negative comments
....	....
....	....
....	....
....	....
....	....
....	....
Tally total	Tally total ....
Words/phrases to watch out for	**Words/phrases to watch out for**
....	....
....	....
....	....
....	....
....	....
....	....

Key ideas summary

Key Idea	Benefit for the LSA	Benefit for the students
The rewards that most students value are relational, not material.	The LSA does not need to spend time and money searching for material rewards.	Students have positive interactions with adults who are sincere with their praise and encouragement.
Acknowledgement and positive reinforcement create a positive ethos in the classroom.	Less time is spent on sanctions and disruptive behaviour. A continually positive ethos gathers momentum.	Students are able to gain your attention through fair means rather than foul!
Praise can be most effective when it is given with subtlety and discretion.	The LSA can reinforce positive behaviour without embarrassing individuals.	Students' communication with the teacher is more personal and effective.
Aim to deliver praise that is sincere and individualised.	You begin to connect with your students and show them your pride in their achievements.	Students appreciate your praise, they recognise when you tailor your praise.
Praise is a far more effective behaviour management tool than sanctions.	Enforcing sanctions is time-consuming and complicated. LSAs have a longer-term impact on behaviour using strategies for praise and reward.	Students are motivated by praise rather than sanctions.

Plan it, write it, do it

Choose a strategy from this chapter to try out. Be realistic about your timescale for implementation and review. It takes at least 30 days to change a habit. Set the criteria by which you will measure the success of the strategy with precision.

Strategy	Resources	Start date	How I will monitor progress	Review date	Success criteria

There is a printable version of the Action Plan on the CD-ROM.

Chapter 7

When Students Break the Rules: Applying Sanctions

'Punishment hardens and numbs, it produces obstinacy, it sharpens the sense of alienation and strengthens the power of resistance.'

Friedrich Wilhelm Nietzsche

The principle

Issuing sanctions is not the responsibility of one individual but of all adults working with students. Your sanctions must be graduated, applied consistently and gently, leaving your relationship with the students untarnished. Students need to be spoken to privately whenever possible, without confrontation or threat. Sanctions must attack the behaviour choice and not the student. A person's behaviour is not their identity. When students choose to break rules that have been taught and made explicit through agreed rules, sanctions need to be applied.

The practice

Don't be surprised when students break your rules and rituals. When they don't reach your high expectations try to take it in your stride. Expect it, plan for it and use it as an opportunity to guide them towards better choices.

Being spoken to about your behaviour in front of your peers is, at best, tense and, at worst, terrifying. Just check your own reaction the next time you are beeped at for some minor driving error, or admonished at the dinner table by your partner in front of friends. Being spoken to about your personal conduct in public is embarrassing; having it shouted across a room full of your peers can be humiliating and more often than not elicits a defensive reaction. So it goes with children.

Private and discreet application of sanctions reduces the risk of challenge and confrontation. The audience is removed and conversation is quieter and calmer.

Names on the board with ticks and crosses make one student's behaviour everyone's business. With older students, systems that publicly highlight behaviour can, in themselves, be a catalyst for disruptive behaviour: e.g. students trying to covertly wipe their names off the board, students laughing at the misfortune of others, public arguments about the level of sanction applied, etc.

There are many non-verbal ways in which you can communicate with the students about their choices before intervening. Your non-verbal cues may not be immediately or accurately understood by a new group of students and you may need to be explicit about the techniques that you are using. For example, 'When I am speaking to the group and I stand next to your table I am giving you a chance to check your choices before I need to stop and give you a verbal warning.' When the group can read your non-verbal cues, your initial response can be discreet yet still have impact. You can begin to manage minor infringements without being interrupted or having to stop what you are saying to others.

Strategy spotlight

Non-verbal cues

Try these strategies.

✔ Stand or sit next to the student as you continue to address the group; it will encourage them to check their behaviour.

✔ Gain eye contact that gently says, 'Come on, let's get back to work,' or a stronger look that indicates that you are aware and disapprove of the behaviour.

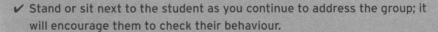

- ✔ Mention the name of a student drifting off task to refocus their attention.

- ✔ Prepare the student to answer a question: 'I have got a question for you Alex. When I have explained this next section to the group I will be asking you about single cell organisms.'

- ✔ Feign shock and surprise at the student's choice of behaviour.

- ✔ Refer to a strong model of the student's previous good behaviour to bring them back on task.

- ✔ Use agreed signals such as miming a writing motion with your hand or placing palms together to ask for books to be closed.

- ✔ Indicate a student's chair with an open palm to invite them to sit down.

- ✔ Stand next to the charts that display the learning rituals and rules and combine eye contact with a finger on the chart to send a clear message.

Over time you will be able to build up a range of non-verbal cues that allow students' poor choices to be addressed subtly within the 'flow' of your teaching. It is these proactive and preventative techniques that are so hard to observe in effective adults, but as they are refined they become more discreet and become so embedded in the teaching style that they are barely noticeable.

Unless it is a serious incident (e.g. verbal abuse directed at an adult, violent behaviour endangering the class) your first sanction should be a verbal warning. Take a moment to prepare what you are going to say to the student. Approach the student calmly and gently and get down to their eye level. Explain that the behaviour witnessed is contrary to the rules or your established expectations and that you are giving them a warning. Then focus on the learning that you expect to see the student engaged in.

If the student tries to divert the conversation or bring in the behaviour of another student, you can say, 'I understand what you are saying, we are talking about . . .,' or, 'I hear that, I am talking about your choices.' You are acknowledging their input to the conversation but returning the focus back to the undesirable behaviour. Finish your discussion by referring to the student's previous good behaviour, 'Last lesson your detailed descriptive paragraph was a result of hard work, try and get back to those good choices,' and leave them feeling positive about the rest of the lesson. You may even add some surprise at the student's poor choices: 'Dan, it is unlike you to need to go down the sanctions route, you are not someone who usually makes poor choices. . . .' Then walk away and look away. Turn your attention to the rest of the class and catch someone doing the right thing. Give the student the space to calm down, consider their next choice and act upon it. After a couple of minutes check that the student who received the sanction is back on task and give them a gentle acknowledgement that you appreciate their better choice. If they are still choosing to break the rules, return and apply your second sanction (often a request for them to see you after class to discuss their behaviour choices) with the same consistent, personal and calm approach.

Refocusing the conversation

When students try to argue, shift the blame or divert the conversation you can either:

- **Calmly and gently repeat the line where you were interrupted.** This shows the student that you will not be diverted from the conversation you are leading. The more calmly assertive you are in delivering this repeat the more effective it will be. I like to soften and slow my speech as I repeat the request. If you repeat the request with frustration it is less likely to have the desired effect. *or*
- **Use an appropriate refocusing line to bring the conversation back to the script.** This allows the student to feel as though they are being listened to and avoids conversational cul de sacs.

Student	Adult
'It wasn't me . . .'	*'I hear what you are saying . . .'*
'But they were doing the same thing . . .'	*'I understand, what I must talk to you about is . . .'*
'I was only . . .'	*'Maybe you were . . . and yet I need to talk to you about . . .'*
'You are not being fair . . .'	*'I can appear unfair, yes, I am hear to talk about . . .'*
'It's boring . . .'	*'Yes, you may be right, I have come here to discuss . . .'*
You are a . . . (name-calling)	*'Maybe that is true, what we must do now is to . . .'* or *'It is a shame you feel that way, we need to pay attention to . . .'*
	[Follow up any personal remarks later in the day/the following morning, rather than chase them in the moment]

How to land a sanction softly

- Remind the student of their previous good behaviour.
- Challenge their negative internal monologue: 'You can do this, you are intelligent and able.'
- Thank the student for listening.
- Position yourself lower than eye level or side on if you are standing; don't demand sustained eye contact.
- Use a soft, disappointed tone.
- Remind yourself that the sanction is a consequence not personal retribution.
- Disconnect the sanction from your emotional state.
- Walk away and give the student space as soon as you have finished speaking.

Although at times it is difficult to separate the two, a student's behaviour is not their identity. Those students who have persuaded adults that their behaviour and identity are inseparable are able to disguise the purity of their core character and divert adults who try to build a relationship. Their behaviour can act as a 'front' to hide behind. When you speak to students about their choices, attack the behaviour and not the student. You can identify and label the behaviour leaving the student's sense of self-worth and self-esteem intact: 'You chose to throw the pen across the room. That behaviour is extremely inappropriate. Think carefully about your next choice of behaviour.'

Watch out for . . .

✔ 'Hovering' by a student after you have applied a sanction. The student needs time and space to make better choices about their behaviour and your continued proximity makes this very difficult. I have observed LSAs who have a graduated sanctions list and, by standing over a student, manage to apply all five sanctions in 30 seconds. The student feels humiliated and resentful. Their personal space has been invaded and they have not been given a fair chance to change their behaviour. A small rules break suddenly escalates into a full-blown confrontation that does not meet anyone's needs.

✔ Holding grudges. Each lesson should be a clean sheet for students. Poor choices in the previous lesson should either be dealt with in the interim or at another time. Students need to know that their identity has not been labelled by their previous poor choices.

✔ Giving a sanction and then taking it away. Regardless of how many good choices the student makes after a sanction is applied you should not remove the sanction. Your students need to understand that there are consequences to certain choices and these are not negotiable. You should reward good choices even if they follow poor ones. It is not unusual for some students to leave the classroom with both.

Reflecting on practice

Instant sanctions with added impact

Working with students who were struggling to control their own behaviour meant that I rarely had lunch alone. I had discovered that having 'guests' to lunch was a highly effective sanction. My acknowledgement, praise and positive reinforcement had most impact when it was immediate. My sanctions needed to match.

For these students the more delayed the sanction the less they associated it with the inappropriate behaviour. Sanctions would simply be an inconvenience in their school week, swiftly integrated into their routine. As a student I remember this well and accepted detention as part of my timetable rather than connecting it with the original behaviour. For me (and a number of my friends) the school day would finish at 4.30 rather than 3.30 and rather than adjust my behaviour I came to accept a later finishing time as an occupational hazard.

For sanctions to be most effective they need to be served immediately and designed to disrupt the student's plan for the day. Holding students at break, lunch and after school works best when lessons fall before their free time or when you are able to collect them before their free time begins. They connect the behaviour directly with the sanction and when their carefully protected and planned free time is compromised they begin to check their behaviour with more care.

Diligent application of impositions (extra work to be completed at home, signed by parents and delivered before school the following morning) can have a similar effect but 'You are in detention a week on Wednesday' is so far removed from the original behaviour that it is questionable whether it really has any impact on future behaviour choices. With students who persistently break the rules you will need to negotiate with parents so that you are able to apply sanctions on the same day as the incident. Students will remind you that you need to give 24 hours' notice before a detention can be served; you can remind them that you have a prior agreement with their parents, pick up the phone and get immediate clearance.

Exercise

Read the sample structure for intervention below and fill in the gaps with examples using vocabulary you are comfortable with. Learn and practise the structure for applying the sanctions below until you are comfortable with the sequence. Don't leave out section 'c' as the strongest model for the behaviour that you expect is the student's previous good choices. This structure is also extremely useful when delivering praise.

(I have included it in *italics*.) In both instances you need to have a structure for opening, developing and closing the interaction efficiently, leaving both parties with their self-esteem intact.

Sample structure for intervention

Key:
Delivering warning/sanction
Delivering praise

a. Gentle approach, personal, non-threatening, eye level, eye contact.

b. State the behaviour that was observed and which ritual/rule it contravenes.

b. *State exactly what it is that you are praising and why.*

    Example: ....

c. Tell the student what the sanction is. Refer to previous good behaviour/learning as a model for desired behaviour.

c. *Tell the student what the reward is.*

    Example: ....

d. Tell the student what will happen if they continue with this approach to learning.

    Example: ....

e. Tell the student that their choice was poor and they need to make better choices.

e. *Thank them for making the right choices.*

    Example: ....

f. Walk away from the student, allowing them time to make a better choice. If they are back 'on task' give them appropriate praise and/or acknowledgement.

g. Scan the room and catch somebody following the routine.

- Do not discuss consequences in learning time. Use 'I understand' or 'I hear what you are saying' and return to you original point.
- Do not allow yourself to be drawn away from the conversation you want to have.
- Recognise secondary behaviours and avoid 'chasing' them (see Chapter 8).

Principles of intervention

- **No judgement is ever made about the student's identity during interventions.** The relationship between LSA and student is paramount and must be protected. People are not their behaviour. Students must take responsibility for their behaviour and not have the opportunity to blame their adults for it.

- **Students are held responsible for the choices they make.** Choice changes the neurochemistry of the brain. You can help the students abandon old neural pathways by creating new ones and then reinforcing them so the old ones fade.

- **Behaviours are shifted to the past tense as soon as possible.** We are not interested in dwelling on poor choices but on creating positive expectations for the rest of the lesson.

- **Presupposition is used to influence students' limiting self-belief.** When unspoken positive assumptions lie behind your language they can affect the student's expectations of their own behaviour.

- **It is essential that scripts are complemented with skilled use of physical language and a tone that is calm, kind and nurturing.** Any script can be undermined by careless physical language or tone that mixes the message.

Using a formal script with students

Using scripts can have a powerful initial impact. To show the students that you have not become teaching robots you will need to counterbalance the negative effects of repetitive instruction. Use high levels of praise but particularly contextual ('That is a GCSE grade C standard piece of work and you are in Year 9. Can I put it on display, please?') and reflective praise ('You must feel great about that design, there is a lot of intelligent thought there'). Depersonalise the negative while keeping the positive relaxed and human.

Students will notice when you move into 'script' mode. It will be a more formal approach, marking the moment for the student. If students start to predict or mimic the script (and they will!) you may choose to ignore it or simply tell them that you are doing it this way so that everyone stays calm and is able to

→

concentrate on their own behaviour. If they are refusing to engage in the process use your 'out-line' (a line you might deliver to stop the conversation that allows you to withdraw with dignity) to regroup.

Sample scripts

First warning (verbal)

'I saw/heard you chose to. . . .' 'You broke rule number. . . .'

'This is a verbal warning.'

'You now have the chance to make intelligent choices.'

'Thank you for listening.'

Second warning (written)

'I saw/heard you chose to. . . .' 'You broke rule number. . . .'

'This is a written warning (accompany this statement with a warning card).'

'Think carefully about your next move. You are in charge of your behaviour and can make intelligent choices.'

'Thank you for listening.'

Third sanction

'I saw/heard you chose to. . . .' 'You broke rule number. . . .'

'This is the third time I have spoken to you. You have chosen to see me for 1 minute after class.'

'................ *(student's name)*, do you remember when .... *(model of previous good behaviour)?* That is the standard of behaviour I expect from you.'

'If you choose to break the rules again you leave me no choice but to park you and issue a detention.'

'Think very carefully about your next move, I know that you can make intelligent choices.'

Thank you for listening.'

Fourth sanction – parking and detention

'I saw/heard you choose to. . . .' 'You have broken rule number. . . .'

'You have chosen to be parked and to receive a detention when we can discuss this calmly.'

Key ideas summary

Key idea	Benefit for the LSA	Benefit for the students
When students break the rules use it as an opportunity to teach them about better choices.	The focus for the interaction is learning about improving choices rather than simply attacking behaviour.	Students are involved in negotiating future expectations rather than just answering for their current behaviour.
Apply sanctions in private whenever possible.	Public confrontations are avoided.	Students have no audience to play to or react for.
Integrate a range of non-verbal cues into the flow of your teaching to prevent inappropriate behaviour.	The LSA is proactive in maintaining the students' attention and does not have to keep stopping to deal with students interrupting.	Students are redirected back to the activity without a fuss or their behaviour being advertised to the rest of the class.
Use a planned framework for intervening and applying sanctions.	The LSA is able to direct and control the direction of the conversation without prompting confrontation.	Students know what to expect, recognise the structure of the intervention and may decide not to argue.
Use students' previous good behaviour as a model for desired behaviour.	The interaction is softened after the sanction is delivered. The conversation ends on a positive note.	Students fully understand the required standards of behaviour.
Use instant sanctions whenever possible.	LSAs can use the time to repair relationships and reinforce appropriate choices while the incident is current. Less time is spent chasing students who are avoiding sanctions for past misdemeanours.	Students are keen to avoid sanctions that eat into their social time without notice.

Plan it, write it, do it

Choose a strategy from this chapter to try out. Be realistic about your timescale for implementation and review. It takes at least 30 days to change a habit. Set the criteria by which you will measure the success of the strategy with precision.

Strategy	Resources	Start date	How I will monitor progress	Review date	Success criteria

There is a printable version of the Action Plan on the CD-ROM.

PART 2

Advanced Behaviour Management Strategies

Chapter 8

Managing Confrontation and Stopping it from Escalating

'I predict a riot.'

Kaiser Chiefs, 'Employment', 2005

The principle

There will be times when, regardless of how well you structure your application of sanctions, you find yourself in confrontation with a student. There will also be times when you are confronted by a student, without warning, for no obvious reason.

The way you manage the confrontation has a direct effect on its outcome, even if the outcome is not an instant solution. A carefully managed confrontation with a student can have positive outcomes even if the beginning of the conversation was a difficult experience for both parties. At all times remember who the adult is, model the behaviour you expect and enjoy skilfully managing the situation to meet the best needs of your students.

The practice

Confrontations can happen in an instant and often when you are least expecting them. You need to work to keep your own emotions in check throughout, to protect yourself and the student. Try to view the confrontation for what it really is, an adult modelling and teaching a child about expected behaviour. I have had many weekends tarnished by guilt after saying the wrong thing to the wrong student late on a Friday afternoon. Stepping back and taking time to consider the most appropriate response is vital if you are to avoid such mistakes.

Your response to the first signs of a confrontation sets the rhythm for the rest of the discussion. Change your focus from being the speaker to being the listener. While you are listening look at your own body language and soften it, take a step back, lower your hands, remove any aggressive tightening of the facial muscles, prepare what you are going to say and wait patiently for your opportunity to say it.

We usually know what our opening sentence will be but few plan beyond it. Work through what you are going to say in response, how you will say it and how you are going to end the conversation, and keep it on track. As with applying sanctions, students need to know that they are being listened to. Use some of the redirection techniques from Chapter 7, 'I hear what you are saying' and 'I understand.' You will find that the confrontation needs the fuel of an equally confrontational response to keep it escalating. If your response is to listen, and keep listening until the student has finished, and then take immediate steps to de-escalate, using appropriate physical and verbal language, any aggression will be short-lived.

Don't try to solve all confrontations instantly. You may need to walk away and take time and advice on how to resolve the situation. You may need to listen, record and then refer on to a senior colleague. When students have sworn, threatened and physically confronted me, I never improved the situation through an aggressive or emotional response.

If you see a confrontation brewing

Try the following:

- Distraction – phone call, urgent message, etc.
- Leading/inviting the student away to a quieter, less public space.
- Removing the audience.
- Listening/not reacting, waiting for the anger to subside.
- Lowering the voice and softening vocal tones.
- Softening your physical language.
- Repeating a key word or phrase, e.g. 'Keep your hands down.'

- Depersonalising the confrontation: 'Try and get control of your anger' rather than 'Get control of yourself!'

- Offering help rather than criticism: 'What do you need me to do?', 'Do you need to be left alone?', 'Would you like to sit down?', 'Is there someone you need to speak to?'

- Asking questions or suggesting alternatives rather than giving advice or instructions.

Strategy spotlight

Anger management

Intensive anger management coaching and counselling can have a marked effect on student behaviour, but providing a diluted version for half an hour a week to groups of students has little chance of success. Educational psychologists identify this as a growing issue for schools that think they are providing appropriate intervention but are unable to give it the time and financial commitment that it requires to have a measurable effect. Students pick up on the fact that the school has given such courses a low priority, and are aware of the frustration that teachers/LSAs feel when students are removed from lessons to attend the course. The intervention can all too easily be undermined by students, 'It's not my fault, I've got anger management problems,' and adults, 'He just uses it as an excuse not to work.' In some cases anger management courses have been misused as a poorly resourced 'final chance' before permanent exclusion: 'He's been on the course, now we can put him out.'

For anger management training to succeed certain conditions and key principles need to be in place.

- Courses are given a high priority by all staff.

- They are well resourced and delivered by trained specialists.

- The course is intensive and one-to-one in the first instance.

- Training is tailored to the needs of the individual student (not simply a series of worksheets).

- The student commits to the course.

- The parents commit to the course and are closely involved and clearly communicated with.

- Everyone is given a clear rationale for the intervention.

- The management of the student is not delegated to the anger management course leader: 'Well, if she can't help him I'm not even going to try.'

- Students are not allowed or encouraged to excuse their inappropriate choices citing 'anger management problems'.

Recording the incident

As soon as possible after the incident make a detailed chronological written record of what happened and who said what. This is not only a useful reflective (and cathartic) action but also clarifies the incident for senior colleagues and parents. If confrontations happen with some frequency carry a Dictaphone or use the voice recorder on your mobile phone to make an accurate verbal record of the incident immediately afterwards (not during it as this can inflame an already tense situation). If appropriate, encourage the student to record their version of events: for younger students call it a 'think sheet' with key questions, e.g. 'What happened to make you feel wound up?, What did you do about this?, What do you think that you should do next time?' Use a cold comparison of the two to learn more about the effect of your actions and reactions on the student.

Some students enjoy a confrontation with an adult. It can be an opportunity for an adrenalin-fuelled interlude in an otherwise uneventful day and is quickly forgotten. Other students try to test their skills and provoking a strong reaction in an adult can be an attractive challenge for a 9/11/15-year-old. For other students confrontation can be frightening and shocking. It can damage the relationship irrevocably. Your careful management of confrontation can quell the former group and protect the latter one.

Watch out for . . .

✔ Chasing secondary behaviours. Students, like adults, have a sophisticated armoury to defend themselves when confronted. A secondary behaviour might be the smirk that glides across the face of a student who is supposed to be looking ashamed, or the chair that is pushed back too hard after the student is sent from the room. These behaviours can attract a stronger response than the initial incident. They are 'chase me' behaviours designed to get an emotional response from the teacher. Don't ignore them but choose the right time to address them when the student has calmed down.

✔ Allowing the discussion to be diverted. There are common diversionary tactics that can extend a 10-second confrontation into an hour-long discussion. They usually start with, 'I don't like this class and my Dad says it's a waste of time anyway,' or, 'What's the point of History?' Use, 'I understand . . .' or, 'I hear what you are saying . . .' to get the conversation back on track.

✔ Bringing up past misdemeanors or using as a model the example of siblings or other students: e.g. 'Your brother never behaved like this.'

✔ Invading students' personal space. Students may feel threatened and become aggressive if their personal space is continually violated.

✔ Making accusations. Use questions instead: e.g. 'Nathan, are you ready to begin?' rather than, 'Nathan, stop playing games on your phone.'

✔ Offering unsolicited advice or criticism when discussing choices with students: 'Do you want to carry on being stupid or have you grown up now?'

Reflecting on practice

Violent behaviour: fights breaking out in lessons

Your skilled management of behaviour and knowledge of individual pupils should minimise physical confrontation between students in lesson time. The culture of mutual trust and regard that you are nurturing will go a long way to reduce the chances of violent conduct. With some extremely volatile students 'hands off' is a useful rule to use while they are learning appropriate behaviour for the classroom. 'Hands off' means no touch in anger or without permission. This has two benefits: it enables you to give a clear command when you see physical confrontation beginning; and it deters those who poke/flick/push others in fun and provoke a violent reaction. With students who are used to this terminology the first flames of aggression can often be extinguished with a loud, low-toned and controlled assertive call of 'DANIEL, HANDS OFF!'

There will be occasions, however, when fights break out. Regardless of your physical size your first move should not be to intervene physically but to send a responsible student to get the nearest adult and in the same breath begin intervening verbally by giving clear instructions to the participants. At this point it is too late to start telling them that you are 'going to get Mr Hopkins' or that 'you will be excluded for this'. Instead your commands should be clear and unassailable: 'Rizwan, put your hands down and step back' or 'Julie McManon, stand still.' If the students are young enough that you can safely physically intervene before another adult arrives then you should do so. As you pull them apart do so by the shoulder or by holding down the arms of one child, so as to keep their arms held to their side. Always guide by the elbows or upper arm and not the wrists. Remember to keep a strong check on your heightened emotional state and ensure that the force you use is the absolute minimum required. Keep talking to the students while you are separating them, explain what you are doing and telling them what you want them to do next: 'I am holding your arms down to stop you hurting anyone,' 'Sit down in the chair.' If you are concerned about restraining

➡

students then the DfES document *Guidance on the use of restrictive physical interventions for staff working with children and adults 2002,* is useful.

With older and stronger students, or those who have lost all emotional control, intervening physically can carry significant risk. If you are in any doubt wait until support arrives and evacuate the room for the safety of other students, leaving the door open. I have witnessed some nasty fights with older teenagers and we have had to wait for five or six adults to arrive before we could be sure of intervening safely. Without support it is all too easy to get involved in the physical to and fro and find yourself being hit, using excessive force, restraining one student while the other takes the opportunity for some 'free hits', or being perceived as showing favouritism to one student over another.

Exercise

Plan your responses to confrontation using the chart. Refer to them throughout the week, adopting them where appropriate. Measure the students' reaction to them carefully.

Responses to confrontation

Your first reaction to an escalating confrontation:

....

While the student is speaking you will:

....

When you want to exit the confrontation you will say:

'..'

As soon as the confrontation has finished you will:

....

When sufficient time has elapsed you will:

....

Key ideas summary

Key idea	Benefit for the LSA	Benefit for the students
Take a step back and listen rather than speak.	The LSA has more time to deliver a considered response; the confrontation is not fuelled from two sides.	Students learn that adults will not engage in aggressive confrontation; they experience a positive model of behaviour at first hand.
Think carefully about what you are going to say and how you are going to say it.	With more considered use of language the LSA has more chance of calming aggression and leading the way out of confrontation.	Students hear simple, impartial instructions and receive non-verbal cues to calm down.
Don't look for instant solutions.	The LSA is not under pressure to improvise an instant resolution and may move the discussion to a more appropriate time/location.	Students are given time to consider their behaviour; they know that 'knee-jerk' or unfair reactions are less likely.
Write a detailed and accurate record as soon as possible.	The LSA has a reliable record of what was said, what took place and who else everyone involved.	The student has the time and space to reflect on the incident before it is discussed.

Plan it, write it, do it

Choose a strategy from this chapter to try out. Be realistic about your timescale for implementation and review. It takes at least 30 days to change a habit. Set the criteria by which you will measure the success of the strategy with precision.

Strategy	Resources	Start date	How I will monitor progress	Review date	Success criteria

There is a printable version of the Action Plan on the CD-ROM.

Chapter 9

Proactively Developing Relationships with 'Hard to Reach' Students

'You can't stay in your corner of the Forest waiting for others to come to you. You have to go to them sometimes.'

A. A. Milne, *Winnie-the-Pooh*

The principle

Students with challenging behaviour select the lessons that they are going to disrupt and teachers/LSAs they are going to frustrate. They find it harder to maintain their aggression and inappropriate behaviour with adults that they trust. There are actions you can take to proactively develop a professional and trusting relationship with an individual student and so reduce their desire for conflict and confrontation when working with you. With particularly challenging students who persistently disrupt and fail to respond to your hierarchy of sanctions the best leverage you have to effect a change in behaviour is to develop a trusting relationship.

The practice

It's not about trying to get down with the kids. Get the image of the LSA in a reversed baseball cap skipping up to a group of gnarled Year 11s with a 'Yo bro, wagwan, dis new Phil Collins is safe, man, big up your bad self' out of your head. It is certainly not what I am suggesting, although it would be fun to watch.

Choose your opportunities to build an initial relationship with a student carefully. Perhaps wait until you see the student away from their peer group, or open up a dialogue when the student appears relaxed and unguarded; chatting in the lunch queue, greeting at the school gates, while involved in extra-curricular activities. You may choose to wait until you find a situation that is not pressured or time limited. Aim for little and often rather than launching into a lengthy and involved conversation.

Gaining trust

Try not to think in terms of gaining the respect or friendship of the student, but about gaining their trust. Trust thrives when two people like each other. It certainly helps if you can get on but trust can and does exist strongly between people who have no real personal connection. It is your responsibility to build trust with all students. It is better to spend your time working on this premise rather than waiting for the students to decide that they are going to bestow their respect on you without question. Some colleagues will busy themselves with mourning the loss of children's respect for adults. Unfortunately it is nearly always a very dull conversation prompted by people who don't really like children and that has no resolution: stay well away.

Of course you may not have the opportunity for preparatory niceties. More often than not you find yourself sitting next to the student in a lesson perhaps having the briefest of introductions. Remember, your attempts to build a positive relationship may be unwelcome at first. Your aim is gently to persuade the student that you are committed to building trust. Be prepared for your approaches to be rejected. The student may be testing you to see how committed to developing the relationship you really are. They may not welcome any informal conversation with you because it is easier for them to deal with conflict than a relationship of trust. Or quite simply, they may have decided that all adults need to be given a wide berth.

Fishing for hooks

Students who are 'hard to reach' may not have an obvious 'hook' or interest that you can key in to. In fact many students will have such low self-esteem that they don't have an interest or feel that they have no potential in any area of their life. Some students will present their interests as only those that promote their status in their peer group; others will tell you they are interested in things designed to shock and worry you. For students who have no obvious 'hook' it can be useful to find and encourage their potential in a certain area or simply to insert a 'hook' in the hope that it will be picked up by the student. For some students you may find it useful to encourage the idea that they have a talent in a certain area even if no discernible ability is obvious. For this to be successful you must drip feed positive reinforcement in a specific area over time. Be prepared for your attempts to hook the student to be rejected. In time the student will question why you keep telling them they have a talent. To reach this moment they will have already questioned their preconceived ideas about themselves and the possibility that they may have talent is tangible. It is less important what the hook is. When students you work with feel that they have potential to succeed in one area it encourages the thought that they may, after all, have the chance to succeed in other areas of their lives as well.

There will be times when you need to seek out the student to deliver a sanction or follow up on an incident. In the early days do not try and use this opportunity to develop your relationship with the student it may send mixed messages. As the relationship develops and you gain a better understanding of each other you may be able to switch between formal and informal registers and still get your message across.

Use informal meetings with parents (Parents' evenings, at the gates, parents' assemblies) to find out a little more about the student's home life, interests and motivations. Weigh up the advantages of accompanying school trips against the obvious disruption to your personal life. Adults who accompany school trips abroad or long weekends away (outward bound, Duke of Edinburgh Award, etc.) often cannot sustain the formal 'mask' that they use in the classroom and are forced to reveal more of their personality to the group. Likewise disruptive students have the same trouble trying to hide the gentler sides of their characters. Adults return from such trips often reporting that their relationship with individuals has changed and developed. They have been more open with each other, without the screen of institutional formality. They have shared experiences which can be used to build the relationship when returning to the school environment. Students may not immediately demonstrate their appreciation for those who invest time in extra-curricular activities but they do recognise the level of commitment and are more likely to give you their trust.

I always loved such trips and volunteered enthusiastically for D of E, skiing in Italy, weekends on Scout camps in Coventry, rainy weekends in Wales ... for me the benefits outweighed the hassles of the bureaucracy, time away from the rest of your life, giving up your weekend, etc. You see the students for who they really are; children learning about a world that is bigger and more exciting than the confines of the institution they work in. Some of the students you work with may not have left the local community to visit even the nearest city. As we attempt to convince some of the harder-to-reach students that they have potential it is important to show them that the world is more dynamic than the four streets that surround the school.

Watch out for . . .

✔ Speaking publicly about conversations you have had privately with students. There is nothing more guaranteed to break trust than blurting out details of informal conversations in the staffroom or in front of other students.

✔ Meeting with students in a closed classroom. Obviously you will need to use your professional judgement and knowledge of the student, but it is always better to meet with students in a public space – school library, dining hall, reception area.

Disclosure

You cannot and never should offer or guarantee pupils unconditional confidentiality. A personal disclosure might occur without warning and when you least expect it. If you suspect that the student is about to disclose sexual abuse, pregnancy, criminal acts, domestic violence, self-harm, forced marriage or any sensitive information that you think needs to be referred onwards, ask them to pause. I find the following script useful:

'I'm sorry to stop you but this is a sensitive issue and I need to tell the principal (or 'named officer'). You can either stop talking to me now and talk to the principal or talk to me and then I will then speak to her. I cannot keep this information confidential. It is not my decision.'

Explain to the student that whilst you appreciate the trust they are giving you there are certain things that you must tell others about. It is part of your responsibility and legal duty.

Once the student has listened to and had an opportunity to think about what you have said they may still wish to disclose sensitive information to you. The DfES guidance here is useful:

'Listen carefully without jumping to conclusions, asking leading questions or putting words into their mouth. Write a record of the conversation as soon as possible distinguishing clearly between fact, observation, allegation and opinion, noting any action taken in cases of possible abuse and signing and dating the note.'
DfES (2004), *Safeguarding Children in Education*

Explain to the student what you will be doing with the information now. Reassure them that at this stage it will only be one other member of staff who knows, and that they will be involved in what happens next. As soon as possible, meet with the designated person or 'named officer' within the school who has responsibility for child protection. If you are unsure as to whom this is, go directly to the headteacher. Thereafter it is not your responsibility to investigate the matter further and if there are repeated disclosures you must repeat the same process.

I have been involved in many cases of personal disclosure and students have rarely been surprised when I stopped them and reminded them of my responsibility to refer the information. In some cases they wanted to release the information and had calculated that telling a trusted teacher was a controlled way of doing so. Sometimes what I thought was a disclosure, particularly on drug and alcohol abuse, was fairly common knowledge outside the institution. Then there were those times when the disclosure was sudden, extreme and urgent. In all cases I am sure that I have acted in the best interests of the child (even if in the short term it has not improved matters) by following the procedures above.

These guidelines are designed to protect the student, yourself and any evidence. They are not a reason for not offering support and guidance to students, and on lesser matters being a confidante. Just as guidance on touch is not designed to stop the to and fro of human interaction so the guidance on safeguarding children should not be viewed as a reason to stop talking and building relationships.

Reflecting on practice

Two sides

Karen was a Year 7 girl who looked as if she was looking for trouble; her reputation went before her. Always angry with the world, dirty, messy and disorganised, she would turn up late every day and sometimes not at all. When she was in class she would swing between being curled up at the back asleep in her coat to fits of rage where furniture and fists would go flying. She was one of those students whose absence makes the day a whole lot easier.

Complaints from staff would flow in and I would leave messages for parents, counsel and confine Karen, and stave off continual requests for her to be excluded. She had recently moved from the local primary school, which had reported a decline in her behaviour and personal hygiene towards the end of her last term. In my numerous discussions with Karen I tried my best to develop a relationship with her, but she wouldn't let me in. She had created a 'front' for school and she was determined not to let it fall.

Some more urgent messages for contact with parents were sent and replied to by letter. Karen insisted that her parents were working all hours and simply didn't have time to come in to school. This written exchange was not improving the situation and

→

phone calls to the house were answered by the grandmother who could offer no help. I resolved to visit the house after work, albeit uninvited.

I arrived at the house and Karen answered. She was not angry but very insistent that she had some things to tell me. As her parents were not in, we agreed to meet during tutor period the next day. It transpired that Karen's parents had left the house some five months ago. She was caring full-time for her elderly and ill grandmother which included broken nights and nights with no sleep at all. She was also running the house, cooking, shopping and cleaning when there was time. She was angry because her parents had left but most of all she was tired. With so much responsibility at home it is not surprising that school was very low on the list of priorities. However the fact that she arrived at school at all was something of an achievement. With additional support Karen managed to get some sleep and more balance in her home/school life. Once the teaching team began to understand the root cause of the problems, they dealt with her with more empathy and care. She responded by controlling her behaviour and finding a channel for her negative energy through sport (though, as I recall, netball became a contact sport for a while). What was so surprising to everyone involved was that as well as hiding her circumstances Karen was hiding a gentle, caring, committed side to her character that was well developed. This was in sharp contrast to the aggression she showed adults and peers. She did not ever complain about having to do the most menial and inappropriate tasks at home yet at school found it a struggle to remove her coat.

Students, like the adults they work with, reveal different character traits at home and at school. In order to proactively develop relationships with students it is often useful to try and blur the separation between the two. Try and find a less formal register to build your relationship; empathy is strength not weakness.

Exercise

Go through the checklist below ticking off those strategies that you already use, selecting three ideas to adopt immediately and three to try over the next few weeks.

 Strategies for proactively developing a relationship with a student

	Already use	Adopt now	Use soon
Make a point of saying something positive as the student enters the classroom.	☐	☐	☐
Make a point of saying something positive as the student leaves the room.	☐	☐	☐

	Already use	Adopt now	Use soon
Identify colleagues who have positive relationships with the student and ask for advice.	❑	❑	❑
Give the student something they may be interested in - a newspaper article, webpage reference, copy of book on loan.	❑	❑	❑
Channel your positive referrals through key colleagues identified above: ensure your message has most impact.	❑	❑	❑
Find specific areas of your work with the student to praise and encourage: 'Your design work is impressive, do you think you might have time to create some images for this display?'	❑	❑	❑
Have lunch at the same table/next to the student.	❑	❑	❑
Seek the student out for an informal conversation.	❑	❑	❑
Ask after the student's welfare, family, football team.	❑	❑	❑
Make a point of saying hello when you pass them in the corridors.	❑	❑	❑
When the student makes good choices let everyone know (loudly in the staffroom if you like).	❑	❑	❑
Phone home with good news about the student's behaviour.	❑	❑	❑
Get eye contact regularly with the student.	❑	❑	❑
Make it clear that you will only judge the student on their current behaviour; past reputation will not negatively influence your expectations.	❑	❑	❑
Respond to changes in their behaviour positively.	❑	❑	❑
Give the student an appropriate responsibility in the classroom - distributing resources, drawing blinds, organising groups, etc.	❑	❑	❑
Make a point of marking work promptly with detailed feedback.	❑	❑	❑

Key ideas summary

Key idea	Benefit for the LSA	Benefit for the students
Challenging students are less likely to misbehave for LSAs with whom they have developed a trusting relationship.	Students who previously disrupted and prevented learning are more willing to listen to you and follow the rules.	Students know that you care enough to go the extra mile. They are unable to hide from the adult world.
Be proactive yet sensitive in slowly developing relationships with students who present challenging behaviours.	The LSA is realistic about the time needed to build a relationship and respectful of the students' right to privacy.	The LSA's approach is safe, unobtrusive and almost nonchalant.
Take advantage of the opportunities that school visits/trips afford for building relationships.	Relationships are built through shared experience, conversations evolve more naturally and outside the tensions of the institution.	Students learn more about their LSAs and are able to interact with them on a less formal basis.
Take care not to send mixed messages, e.g. by delivering sanctions while trying to build your relationship.	The LSA holds the application of sanctions separate from informal conversations. The developing relationship is not abused.	The student understands that the LSA's high expectations of behaviour remain constant.
Follow agreed school procedures for 'disclosure'.	The relationship is protected and confidentiality is not assumed.	The student is given clear information about the consequences of disclosing sensitive information.
Spending time with the students out of lessons in social areas affords you more time to develop positive relationships.	There are more opportunities for informal conversation; you get to know students without the pressures of the classroom.	Students are able to open up dialogues that are not focused on class work.

Plan it, write it, do it

Choose a strategy from this chapter to try out. Be realistic about your timescale for implementation and review. It takes at least 30 days to change a habit. Set the criteria by which you will measure the success of the strategy with precision.

Strategy	Resources	Start date	How I will monitor progress	Review date	Success criteria

There is a printable version of the Action Plan on the CD-ROM.

Chapter 10

Building Mutual Trust

'You can discover more about a person in an hour of play than in a year of conversation.'

Plato

The principle

Although achieving mutual trust between students, and between adults and students, is a high expectation to set, it is not an unreachable ideal. A learning environment that has mutual trust between learners is a place where risks can be taken and thoughts drafted aloud. Fear of public failure is reduced and students engage in sustained bouts of higher-order thinking. Creating mutual trust should not be an add-on to your behaviour management, but a core function of a successful learning relationship. In order to create an environment where trust can be nurtured there must be opportunities for students to resolve conflict, complain when trust has been violated and engage in learning activities where trust is given and received.

The practice

It is not about respect but about trust. Before you are able to give respect you must give and receive trust. Defining trust for, and with, the students you work alongside is an important first step. Students use a variety of terms for highlighting trust. Although their language is probably different from yours, students' vocabulary has established definitions within their friendship groups and at home. Don't reject their language or definitions, but mix in your own ideas to write up or map out a collective definition of trust. Display it prominently.

Your modelling is critical. There are concrete actions that you can take to encourage mutual trust between learners. Try asking for student feedback on your teaching on a regular basis. You may choose to give a formal evaluation or engage in a series of less formal and more private conversations with students. Make a point of refusing to allow students to lose face in public, regardless of their behaviour. If you encourage behaviour covertly by ignoring the comments of other students you are providing a poor model of appropriate behaviour. Avoid ridiculing students or using labels or derogatory nicknames and establish firm sanctions for students who name call or put down others. There are many adults who amuse themselves by allocating sarcastic and derogatory nicknames for their students. They may think that this is a way of 'connecting' with them or of injecting some humour into their day. In reality students can become confused about your sincerity and quickly tire of being called 'Speedy', 'Clown' or 'Scruff'. Laugh *with* your students regularly, not at their expense, and check your immediate response to students who make mistakes in public.

There are principles you can adopt that both LSAs and students can take to strengthen trust.

LSAs	Students
We are consistent and predictable.	Our words match our actions and we keep promises.
We communicate accurately, openly and honestly.	We talk through difficulties openly.
We share and delegate control.	If you give trust then you will receive it.
We demonstrate empathy and understanding.	We show concern for others.
We perform competently.	We do our best work, particularly when other people are relying on us.

Practical strategies for building mutual trust

✔ Nurture a common identity for groups of students creating a sense of unity. In talk and actions use 'we' rather than 'you'.

✔ Establish or agree joint goals that are clearly defined, shared and displayed.

✔ Model and teach active listening. Demonstrating appropriate verbal and physical language for a listener, modelling appropriate responses, paraphrasing and checking back with the student: 'So what I think you are saying is. . . .'

✔ Value work by displaying it and involving students in design and creation. Find a space in the classroom/library/staffroom/ that you can use to display students' work ('Paul's Quality Selection').

✔ Make time for informal conversation (over lunch, playing games, as a reward for a sustained period of work) while clearly defining the differences between formal learning time and social time.

Encouraging mutual trust

At primary level, students' mutual trust is encouraged through sharing and delegating jobs in the classroom. A well-organised Year 3 class will have students handing out resources, clearing and cleaning the room, preparing areas for different activities, drawing blinds, etc. The students learn how to share responsibility with others and accept responsibility for themselves. It is often said that primary schools teach students to be independent and secondary schools teach them not to be. Year 7 students in their new schools are often surprised when their responsibility for the classroom is removed – 'Right, *I* am counting out the scissors and *I* will come round hand them out, don't touch them until I say' – and their freedom of movement restricted – 'Do not get out of your seat without written permission!' etc. The tasks and responsibilities that you are able to share may seem mundane and trivial but an ethos of shared responsibility is given a secure foundation.

When trust is violated it can have a negative effect on behaviour, performance and results. Trust violations stifle mutual support and need to be dealt with as soon as possible. As students develop their skills in reconciliation, you will need to take the lead in discussions on repair and reparation. Before you bring the two parties together, make sure that you have accurate written accounts or precise verbal reports. Insist on sincere, polite communication between the students and be prepared to reconvene the meeting if this cannot be achieved quickly. Negotiate or provide students with clear choices on restitution and/or penance and help them to renegotiate their expectations for the future. Encourage students to reaffirm their commitment to building a trusting relationship.

Watch out for . . .

✔ Ignoring violations of trust. By ignoring these you are risking a problem festering, growing and re-emerging as a more complex conflict.

✔ Students who persistently violate trust and/or seem unable to give trust. These students will need additional support and their behaviour may be a sign of more complicated issues outside of the classroom.

Reflecting on practice

The kangaroo court of Judge Dix

Alistair was a highly intelligent student with quirky mannerisms and a slightly eccentric outlook. Other students were wary of him, he had few friends and was outcast from the to and fro of social interaction. The rest of the students in the class were not challenging in their behaviour towards him but as a matter of course would disregard his views, laugh openly at him and tease him relentlessly, although not with intended malice. His status within the group was at an all-time low, his work was slipping from its high standard and it was clearly time for me to show some more public support.

Lessons with this group were good-humoured and amiable. We enjoyed our work, classes were rigorous, challenging and I felt comfortable in taking risks. Over a period of time I instituted a system of reparation for 'crimes' committed by students over the course of the week. These were not behaviours that broke the rules or were connected directly with learning but were minor misdemeanours (often invented) that I would record and list, and then distribute related forfeits for in the last lesson on a Friday.

Taking Alistair aside one day I discussed the possibility of giving this evolving game a structure, a makeshift court with me as the judge and Alistair as my chief prosecution lawyer. It would, after all, help with some of our work on *To Kill a Mockingbird* and be most entertaining to boot. The following day he arrived complete with wig, gavel and a sign that must have taken him most of the evening to create. He adapted to his new role with aplomb, developing advanced 'legalese' and modelling accurate speech structures for the courtroom.

We tried cases such as 'the Crown v Kirsty Appleton – the case of the broken pencil' or 'the Crown v Mark T – internet plagiarism or original thought?' There was never any real justice as I would always twist and subvert the verdict and summary sentence, and the students enjoyed this good-humoured 'kangaroo' justice. We had no end of volunteers to act as the accused, defence lawyers, jury and witnesses for both sides. Everyone was keen to get involved and as Alistair's performance improved week on week, his status in the class grew. The other students began to understand what made him tick and were more willing to put their trust in him. They could see his skill and enthusiasm in action rather than hidden in his lengthy essays.

Slowly the teasing and laughing stopped and they began consulting him about impending cases and learning useful linguistic structures for their own speeches. They eventually (and quite rightly) convinced him to organise a *coup d'état* placing me on trial at the end of the term, and taking the judge's seat himself. The students had begun to understand Alistair and me a little more. My trust in him had proved a good model for the class.

Exercise

Trust exercises sit comfortably alongside long-established frameworks for trust building such as 'circle time'. They are used in the theatre to quickly establish mutual physical trust between actors. These exercises:

- immediately identify barriers to giving and receiving trust;
- actively involve students in using strategies to promote trust;
- throw up questions and ideas about self-discipline;
- encourage students who rarely work together to build trust;
- highlight students who have difficulty giving and receiving trust on a one-to-one basis;
- are fun, thoroughly enjoyable and rewarding.

When I am leading a session on trust it is always made clear to the students that if they do not follow the rituals they will be asked to sit out immediately (and later reintegrated) as the safety of students is the highest priority. Establish your learning ritual early and implement it vigorously. When the atmosphere in the room is really focused, the exercises are tense, exciting and revealing. It is a good idea to start with the first activity and build up in small steps, perhaps using each one as a rung on a 'ladder of trust'.

Some of the activities outlined below can be run in a classroom; others need more space. There are more advanced trust exercises such as 'falling' and 'leaping into a sea of arms' but they need to be explained physically rather than read and interpreted. The origins of these exercises can be found in Clive Barker's *Theatre Games*.

Initiate a 'stop' signal for the whole group and between students. Try a shortened countdown in case you want to stop them quickly and encourage students to use their partner's name as well as 'stop': e.g. use 'Ewan, stop' to differentiate commands from pairs working nearby.

1. Leading the blind

In pairs, A and B, students lead each other using a tie or piece of string. A holds the string in both hands with eyes tightly shut while B slowly leads him around the room, avoiding contact with the rest of the participants. The As are attempting to give trust by keeping their eyes open and the Bs are receiving trust and trying to use it responsibly. Experiment with shorter and longer leashes, leading around objects and in controlled conditions over obstacles.

2. Trust cars

Again in pairs, A with eyes shut and B leading but this time from behind – A is the 'car' and B the 'driver'. To begin with there are three agreed signals: hand on the left shoulder turn left (and keep turning until the hand is removed), hand on the right shoulder turn right (ditto) and flat hand placed (gently!) between the shoulder blades to stop. As the exercise develops students will naturally develop other ideas for useful controls. B 'drives' A around the room and trust is seen to be broken if B opens his eyes.

3. Walking into walls

A and B stand opposite each other 7 to 8 metres apart. With eyes closed A will walk towards B and only stop when the command is given. If the command is late, or A walks too fast, the two will collide. Model the exercise to show how long it takes for the command to be registered and the walker halted. Extend this exercise for responsible students so that the walker speeds up or is heading towards the wall rather than his partner.

Key questions

Weave in some key questions for students to discuss in preparation for the exercises or as reflection:

- How do we give trust?
- How do you receive trust?
- What stops trust building?
- What helps you give and receive trust?
- What can you do to encourage trust?
- What kinds of trust do we need in the classroom?

Key ideas summary

Key idea	Benefit for the LSA	Benefit for the students
Map a collective definition of trust with your students.	A common language and understanding is used in the classroom; the display useful to refer to.	Student language and definition of ideas is given status.
Do not allow students to be publicly ridiculed.	You can remain impartial and fair.	The learning space is free from humiliation, the LSA can be trusted to provide support when necessary
Nurture a common identity with groups of students, identify shared goals.	Responsibility for learning and target setting is shared. High expectations are defined and sustained.	Students have a responsibility to each other and a voice in defining a shared vision.
Laugh with your students and not at them.	The LSA does not casually risk damaging their relationship with any student.	Students understand that their LSA has a sense of humour, not just a cruel streak.
Establish a simple procedure for repairing violations of trust.	Incidents are dealt with calmly and efficiently; conflicts between students or between LSAs and students are not allowed to grow.	Students have responsibility for repairing and maintaining trust.
Share responsibility for learning and organising the classroom with students.	The LSA has more time to dedicate to students. The learning space is more efficiently organised.	Students learn to mange their own learning independently and responsibly. They feel that they are trusted.

Plan it, write it, do it

Choose a strategy from this chapter to try out. Be realistic about your timescale for implementation and review. It takes at least 30 days to change a habit. Set the criteria by which you will measure the success of the strategy with precision.

Strategy	Resources	Start date	How I will monitor progress	Review date	Success criteria

There is a printable version of the Action Plan on the CD-ROM.

PART 3

Collaborating with Other Adults

Chapter 11

Seeking Support: Why, When and How

'A hoot like an owl means all right. Three hoots means something's up.'

Swallows and Amazons, Arthur Ransome

The principle

It is your right to seek support from class teachers, senior staff and parents when necessary, but you need to manage this support carefully. If you always delegate responsibility for managing the behaviour of students to colleagues it will weaken your relationship with the individual, your status and authority. You have a responsibility to remain a part of the management of even the most challenging students, even if that student has been removed from the class and is being dealt with by someone else. However, you also have a right to be protected, trained and mentored as you learn and refine your behaviour management skills and strategies.

The practice

Reality checkpoint

It goes something like this . . . A student behaves appallingly while working with you. The class teacher and then senior manager is called for. With your emotional brain only just in check, you explain what has happened and the student is taken away to receive appropriate punishment. You return to your work, satisfied that the student has been disciplined, and try to calm yourself and the rest of the students down. The next time you see this student is at the start of your next session together. The student enters holding a report card and refuses to engage with you or the lesson. Another incident occurs and support is summoned and again removes the student. You complain that nothing has changed and the support you have received is not solving anything. You even start to believe that the student in question is 'unteachable' and there is a general grunt of agreement over mugs of tea in the staffroom. The student clearly resents the way that he has been treated and most of his resentment is directed at you.

If you ask for support make sure that you stay involved in the process, conversations and negotiations about returning to the group.

Calling on support – reactive

If your call for support is because of persistent, low-level disruption make sure that you have calmly exhausted a range of strategies and at each stage given the student the space and time to make better choices. Your call for support should be a rational response and not one born out of your own frustration. If you are calling for support because of a single incident of extreme behaviour don't try and address it with the student when support arrives: wait until everyone has had longer to calm down and reflect on what has happened.

There will be times when you simply need to pass a student on to another member of staff but there are concrete benefits to your working life in following up the incident later.

Why you should follow up incidents personally

- The professionals who are best placed to have an impact on the behaviour of the student are the LSA and class teacher.
- Senior colleagues cannot control the behaviour of students remotely.
- The student may come to the next session with resentment if difficulties have not been resolved.
- You have a responsibility to build relationships with every student regardless of their individual needs or current behaviours, or whether you like them or not.

- You have a responsibility to talk to the student about their behaviour, take the lead in repairing trust and reinforce high expectations for the next time you meet. This is a strong model of appropriate behaviour.

- If you persistently pass responsibility to a colleague the student begins to imagine that you are not able to manage their behaviour.

- Many students with chaotic home lives are testing whether the adults around them are going to give up and pass them on to someone else.

- You may discover information about the incident or background to it that will prove useful when managing the student in future.

- Colleagues see that you are committed to managing the behaviour of all students: when you ask for support it is more likely to be provided enthusiastically.

Think carefully about the process you go through before calling for a colleague to sanction or remove a student that you are working with. Colleagues will rightly be suspicious if you regularly call on them within the first few minutes or if they need to return to your working area every five minutes throughout the lesson to speak to the student. It is easy to infer from this that you wish to pass responsibility for managing the behaviour of your students to a third party. This won't go down too well in the staffroom or with the colleagues who are being delegated to.

When your colleague arrives to help, speak to them privately and discreetly, preferably away from the student in question. Try to be flexible in the support requested from your colleague. It may not be possible or indeed appropriate for the student to be removed for the whole lesson or even part of it. Often the arrival of another member of staff who can support high-level sanctions is enough to encourage the student to modify their behaviour. Keep your conversation calm – focused on observed behaviours and non-judgemental. Try asking for advice rather than demanding specific and immediate actions. Weigh up your next move carefully:

- Do you really want the student removed or is there a chance that they may be able to rectify their behaviour?

- What outcome are you trying to achieve?

- What, if anything, do you want the supporting teacher to reinforce?

If the student is removed from the lesson make time before the next lesson with the same class to speak to the student calmly and quietly, preferably with the supporting colleague at the meeting. This meeting is vital. Make the time for it and the investment will pay off. Don't be put off by the number of other incidents the student may have been involved in that day or find excuses not to convene it. Your primary concern should be the student's behaviour when working with you. Try dropping in on their tutor period or arranging to have five minutes with the student out of a colleague's lesson.

By meeting with the student, calmly explaining why they had to be removed and what behaviour you expect to see from them next time, you are sending a clear message to the student: you want them to be a part of the group, you care about their learning and you are responsible for the behaviour of all students you work with. This message may not filter through in the first instance but over time it will become clear. You will feel involved in their reintegration and your relationship with them will develop. You will be able to refer to the conversation you have had in future incidents and other students will begin to understand that you use support from other colleagues as a temporary measure and not as a permanent attempt at a solution.

Calling on support – proactive strategies

Who to ask for support

When planning the support that you would like consider carefully which colleagues are best placed to help. Your first port of call will naturally be the class teacher. If this is not the case or you feel that you would like more support than they can offer then it is worth taking time to consider who can be most effective. If can often be tempting to seek out the most senior teacher who holds the key to the most severe sanctions, but there are other angles you can take. It may be worth going to a member of staff whom the student holds in high regard and speaking to them. In addition to a clear insight into the student's behaviour this colleague may also be able to discuss issues informally with them, recommend you as 'one of the good ones' and 'drop by' at a useful moment. This may be a senior colleague but equally it may be another LSA, support worker, class teacher or peripatetic teacher.

What information to take

Before you ask for support from a colleague record the behaviour of the student over a series of lessons so that you have detailed information to present. Trying to support a colleague who gives only a verbal report on what has been happening over the past week/month/term with a student is a tricky business. Once verbal information is translated to the student it can become unspecific and blurred, and does not contain the detail needed to block the defensive responses: e.g. 'But I never said that, it wasn't like that, that was Trevor not me.'

What form would you like the support to take?

Don't leave the support that you receive to chance. Decide what kind of support you would like to receive and in what form before you meet with the colleague. Do you want additional training, resources, changes in grouping, behaviour coaching or changes in timetable allocation? There may be ideas that come out of the meeting but there is no harm in guiding the discussion. Consider having meaningful outcomes that support your work in the short, medium and long term.

How are you going to follow up the meeting?

Agree when and where the follow-up to the initial meeting will take place. Send a reminder about the follow-up meeting at least three days before it is due to happen. Agree an agenda for this meeting in light of progress on the agreements.

Keeping accurate records

Keeping accurate, dated and detailed records on student behaviour means that you have valuable evidence that can be used in a variety of ways to support your requests for additional internal support and:

- to look for patterns of behaviour – days of the week, times in the day;
- to share with parents;
- to share with the student;
- to support school requests for support from external agencies.

It can, however, be very time-consuming to make accurate records of each student and you may find it better simply to begin making detailed records on individuals as soon as you notice sequences of poor behaviour.

How are you going to record agreements that are made?

You may choose to write an action plan following or during the meeting, take minutes, send a follow-up email confirming the agreements made. Ensure that you have a written record of the steps everyone has agreed to take. In a busy work environment, today's undertaking can easily become forgotten in tomorrow's emergencies. Use the record as a working document to record your progress and bring it to the follow-up meeting to check agreements have been honoured.

Watch out for . . .

✔ Deferring responsibility to senior mangers too quickly, too often or too publicly: 'When your head of faculty hears about this . . .' or 'I'm going straight to the Head'. It can make you appear desperate and weak.

✔ The student who has been excluded from school after an incident while working with you. His feelings of resentment are likely to be stronger and he will have had a greater input from senior colleagues and parents. Ask to be a part of the reintegration process and the negotiations with the student even if the exclusion is bundled with other incidents.

✔ Only seeking support for negative behaviours. Forewarn and negotiate with senior colleagues so that you can send students to them for praise or ask them to drop into your session to deliver praise. Focus particularly on those students who, having made poor choices, then make a decision to work hard.

Reflecting on practice

Common procedures and responsibilities

Schools and colleges should and do have set procedures for calling a colleague, usually a senior member of staff, to an incident in a lesson. What is not often discussed is the management of the arrival of the 'on call' teacher.

The following list of responses was generated by 120 teachers and LSAs on a training day after enacting and reflecting on appropriate use of support.

What the LSA can do before the supporting teacher arrives

- Remove the student from the situation, if appropriate.
- Quietly ask the student to pack things ready to leave.
- Back off, don't continue the confrontation/discussion.
- Keep in mind that the student's behaviour is not a personal attack on you and that the sanction is the result of their poor choices.
- Remember, students need to be removed to give them the time and space to calm down, not as a punishment in itself.

LSAs' responsibilities

- Don't discuss the behaviour publicly either in front of the student or in front of the arriving teacher.
- Model appropriate behaviour by remaining calm.
- Have the conversation with the teacher in private.
- Don't take the bad behaviour personally (even if it is personal you may just be in the wrong place at the wrong time).
- Think about your responsibility for the situation: how can you address the problem in future lessons?.
- Speak personally to the student about the incident at a later date.
- Set a positive target for future behaviour.
- Only ask things of the teacher that they will be able to deliver.
- Keep the explanation of the incident brief and to the point.
- Record strategies that you have used with the student before resorting to calling for support.
- Do not use the arrival of a colleague to publicly vent your anger at all the ills of all the students you are working with: '. . . and Boyce has been just as bad, yes you and your mate Jez neither of you have done anything since September . . . , etc., etc.'

Responsibilities of the teacher who comes to offer support

- Approach the situation calmly.
- Model good behaviour for the rest of the class.
- Reinforce good behaviour in others through praise.
- Explain to the rest of the class why the disruptive student is being removed.
- Don't undermine the LSA.
- Listen carefully to what the LSA tells you about the incident.
- Don't judge the situation there and then, ask for accurate records.

Exercise

Photocopy the chart below and either attach it to your school's incident report sheet or use it as a standalone resource. When an incident occurs that requires the support of a colleague, hand the checklist to them so that they can see the strategies that you have used with the student. This checklist is useful as an *aide-mémoire* for yourself and a prompt sheet when discussing the incident with the student after the lesson. It also serves to remind colleagues that you are using positive behaviour management techniques and places the responsibility for the incident firmly with the student.

Behaviour management strategies used

Acknowledged good behaviour choices ☐

Spoke to the student privately and on eye level ☐

Was consistent in application of my behaviour plan ☐

Gave the student time and space to rectify behaviour ☐

Listened to the student ☐

Referred to the learning rituals ☐

Gave a verbal warning

.... sanction given ☐

.... sanction given ☐

Student was moved away from friends ☐

Used positive reinforcement to get the student back on task ☐

Drew back from confrontation ☐

Student given 'time out' to calm down ☐

Key ideas summary

Key idea	Benefit for the LSA	Benefit for the students
LSAs have responsibility for the students in their care; this responsibility cannot be delegated or passed over.	The leadership of behaviour management is not undermined by the delegation of responsibility.	Students know that they are accountable to the LSA for their behaviour in class.
When incidents occur make time to meet with the student and renegotiate expectations.	The LSA is able to reinforce the rules of the classroom and build an understanding of the student's needs.	Students are certain that poor choices in behaviour will be followed up. They have an opportunity to have their say.
Ensure that before you call for support you have calmly and fairly applied your framework for behaviour management and exhausted positive strategies.	When colleagues understand that you are using positive strategies and structured interventions they are able to feel confident in offering the support requested.	Students are treated according to the agreed framework for behaviour management; when support is called it is clear to everyone that it is necessary.

Plan it, write it, do it

Choose a strategy from this chapter to try out. Be realistic about your timescale for implementation and review. It takes at least 30 days to change a habit. Set the criteria by which you will measure the success of the strategy with precision.

Strategy	Resources	Start date	How I will monitor progress	Review date	Success criteria

There is a printable version of the Action Plan on the CD-ROM.

Chapter 12

Teaching Partnerships: Collaborative Approaches with the Class Teacher

'Loneliness is never more cruel than when it is felt in close proximity to someone who has ceased to communicate.'

Germaine Greer

The principle

There is strength in numbers. If the adults within the room are speaking with one voice, are consistent in their application of strategies and are committed to the same goals, the management of behaviour is streamlined. If an adult is poorly briefed or uses behaviour management techniques that are not in line with those of the other adult(s) then the classroom quickly becomes divided. Some students will take advantage of the divide.

The practice

Before you begin work in a new classroom it is worth the extra time and effort to have a formal meeting with the teacher. I know that this is not always so easy and that some teachers will welcome meeting with you while others will retreat to their safe place and hide! This meeting is vital however not just to gain an insight into their subject, module of work and teaching style but for some simple agreements to be made on the management of behaviour. Assuming that you will be in the class fairly regularly you need a voice in the classroom that can develop to an equal status. It is not in anyone's best interests to leave LSAs trying to employ their own strategies in isolation.

Your management of adults in the classroom is worth the investment of time. I realise that it seems easier to nod a hello and then sit at the back trying to stop Darren and his friends chewing the curtains, but it is a false economy. Organise a regular time when you can sit down and talk to the class teacher, even if this is 10 minutes over coffee every Thursday morning. Plan to discuss key behaviour strategies in each meeting as well as the immediate business of lesson content, groupings and responsibilities. This needs to be a two-way conversation, and alongside following your own agenda, you should be listening to feedback on how your work is developing. The perspective of the LSA is unique; you often receive the lesson with the students and see their private reactions to it. If the class teacher is open to it you can suggest adjustments to the lesson while offering your support for individuals.

Although some teachers that you will work with may have a large repertoire of behaviour management skills, some will have had little training in practical strategies. Starting from simple agreements, a collaborative approach can make a huge difference to how other adults perceive their role and feel empowered to take responsibility for managing behaviour. As a member of the teaching team in the classroom you need to invest time in training and sharing strategies and techniques that work with your students.

Raising your status

If the teacher is the only one that gives out rewards and sanctions other adults will be viewed as of lower status. If you can raise your status to one that is equal to the teacher's, you will be laying a solid foundation on which to build positive behaviour strategies and the students will benefit from learning with two confident, assertive adults.

10 ways to raise your status

✔ Know what is going to be taught in the lesson.

✔ Reserve the right to apply all sanctions.

✔ Join in with class discussions.

✔ Be vigilant of the students who are within your radar. Be proactive in managing behaviour.

✔ Give instructions to the whole class – have a voice as part of a teaching partnership.

✔ Be open about your support for the class teacher, even when you disagree.

✔ Set high expectations and model them.

✔ Be available for any student to come and show you their work.

✔ Take part/lead lunchtime clubs, extra-curricular activities, school visits.

✔ Never discuss students negatively in the staffroom.

The balance of power should change when there is more than one significant adult in the room. Suddenly there are less hiding places for those trying to avoid engaging in the lesson. There are fewer dark corners as the adults work the room, managing behaviour and learning as a team. Student to staff ratio is halved and, used successfully, additional staffing can reduce the number of students who need your attention and the number who disrupt.

'Stick with him, don't let him out of your sight'

You may have a remit to work with one individual and at times be discouraged from joining in with the rest of the class. Although some students welcome this one-to-one interaction, it can become frustrating for them if they are always sitting and working with the same adult. Their separation from the rest of the class can be intensified, and it is easy for them to feel that they are being continually watched and guarded. It is important that adults who are supporting individual students have time away and opportunities to work with others in the class. This is not to undermine their role with the individual, as this will remain their primary focus, but to give both parties time apart and allow the student to engage in independent thought, learning and socialisation. If an LSA is attached to a student for every lesson then neither has the space to develop their own learning and practice. In time it can feel as though the LSA and the student exist in a different world to the rest of the class. You begin to feel like a ghost who moves around from class to class only ever noticed by one student. The adults stop communicating as they have distinctly different roles; other students ignore you as you don't impact on their world.

> **Creating a warning mechanism**
>
> If your class teacher feels that they should maintain control over higher-level sanctions (either temporarily or permanently) you will need to agree a level at which the students' behaviour is referred to them. Create a subtle mechanism to inform the class teacher when students reach, say, level 4 on your sanctions hierarchy: pass a note, whisper the student's name, write a note on the desk, ask for the 'purple pen', etc. Discussing such instances in front of the student/class risks confrontation or unwelcome intervention from other students.

Managing difficult teachers!

Working in a classroom with a teacher who is failing to meet the needs of the students presents a range of challenges and frustrations for the LSA. Even when the status and authority of the class teacher are challenged and the balance of power shifts there are strategies you can employ to protect yourself and the students working with you. If you want to engage teachers in a productive discussion about the classroom management skills then the principles we use to encourage positive responses and appropriate behaviour from the students can be applied. With your language, attitude and approach tailored to the recipient and your 'eggshell-walking' skills honed you can make progress with even the most awkward of characters!

Working in a classroom that has no functioning behaviour plan, with a class teacher who struggles to maintain order, is a stressful experience. As you try to encourage students to concentrate on their work they are distracted and attracted by more interesting capers. Your position is a difficult one, stuck between a teacher who is failing to manage behaviour effectively and students who recognise a weakness and seek to exploit it. On the one hand you must show loyalty and demonstrate consistency, and on the other your students are used to your honesty and insight. How can you pretend that everything is all right when it is obvious to everyone that there is a real problem? How can you be proactive and work to improve the situation when you have a limited influence?

You have a unique and unbiased view of how teaching is received; an accurate sense of the rhythm of inappropriate behaviour. Despite this your reflections may not be welcomed as teachers in trouble may have a number of reasons for not wanting to address their obvious training needs. They may be fully aware of the situation they find themselves in or blissfully ignorant. Either way your direct approach may not be welcomed or have the desired effect. More subtle strategies may well protect everyone:

10 ways to encourage the class teacher to address behaviour management issues

✔ Ask for advice, help, training – even if you don't particularly need it yourself you are encouraging the class teacher to reflect on their own knowledge of the subject.

✔ Give time to listen. Initiate discussion that is not class specific: 'Do you think behaviour is getting worse?' etc. Try to understand their approach/philosophy. However much you disagree with most of it, search for common ground.

✔ List strategies that work with particularly challenging students. These might be strategies that you use or ones that colleagues find useful; send them to the class teacher for feedback.

✔ Establish your own behaviour radar and discuss how to do this with the teacher

✔ Leave this book lying around so that it might be 'discovered'.

✔ Ask if you can help design and manage a behaviour management display so that 'students know we are serious'.

✔ Offer to help monitor certain pupils over the course of six lessons using a 'class report' format, make sure this is sent to the class teacher and line manager (see the CD-Rom).

✔ Catch the class behaving appropriately and publicly reinforce this with the students: 'I just wanted to say how pleased we are with the students in this area of the classroom today.'

✔ Stand at the door of the room, welcoming the students as they enter (with or without the teacher), modelling a positive approach at all times

✔ Catch individual students doing the right thing and inviting the class teacher to join in with praise and positive reinforcement

Bad news sandwiches

If you choose to take a more direct approach with the class teacher then 'sandwich' the negative feedback in between positive reflections on how the class/teaching is progressing. Limit yourself to one piece of bad news each time and one action that you would like to move forward with:

'I thought that you may have had a small breakthrough with Adam yesterday. His face lit up when you gave him the credit. Can we try using more positive reinforcement with Yusuf? I think he is getting tied up in arguments with staff and maybe we could break this emerging cycle if we act quickly. Did you notice how well Kaylea did after you moved her away from Charlene? That was a good move.'

The balance of the conversation is with the positive reflections, the bad news sits comfortably between them and is less likely to be received badly or responded to defensively.

Watch out for . . .

✔ Threatening students with a higher authority than the class teacher: 'I'll tell the deputy head about this.'

✔ Being drawn into public three-way confrontations between student and teacher.

✔ Making sure you model appropriate behaviour for the students. This includes: turning up on time, with appropriate equipment and mobile phone switched off; not leaving the classroom during the lesson; listening when one person is speaking to the class.

Reflecting on practice

When other adults take over – a lesson observed

The start of the lesson was fairly calm, a struggle with quiet but nothing out of the ordinary. I had already noted how quiet the teacher's voice was and was interested in how the class was responding to her. There was off-task behaviour but it was not noisy and the pockets of disturbance were kept fairly isolated. As I wondered if her vocal softness was a deliberate ploy or not, the door flew open. Things were about to get a whole lot louder.

Addressing the boys at the back from the door the LSA cut across the whole class and began her behaviour management strategy. This, it turned out was to confront each and every misdemeanour with the tone and physical language that you would avoid witnessing on the streets. The teacher had no chance. All attention was on the LSA who would launch into aggressive personal attacks on the boys at the most inopportune moments. The tension in the room was palpable as some of the larger boys became genuinely affronted by the attacks which were given an anti-male bias: 'You going to be a stupid boy for ever, yes boy, you ain't no man, etc.' The rest of the class tried to shield themselves from the explosions and the teacher was left ignored and unheard. I was dumbfounded and was finding it difficult to remain the silent observer. It soon became clear, however, that this lesson was no different to the ones that had gone before. The LSA knew that intimidation worked for her outside the school gates and saw no reason why it should not work within them. She was indeed a frightening presence in the room.

In discussion with the teacher and LSA, I discovered that the two had never met to discuss roles in the lesson, and that the present situation had been going on for a number of weeks. The teacher felt that she needed more time to develop strategies that worked for her while the LSA, frustrated by the teacher's lack of control, had decided to do it her way. The result for the students was a learning environment that was tense and unproductive. Balancing the responsibilities between the two in a formal agreement was the first step to repairing the damage and finding a workable way forward.

Many LSAs find themselves forced to guess what is expected of them in classrooms. It is hardly surprising that they can act inappropriately when thrown in at the deep end. Giving time to sit down and discuss a strategy for collaboratively managing the behaviour in the classroom really is time well spent.

Exercise

Use the list opposite to generate discussion, introduce basic strategies and create a simple agreement between all of the adults working in your classroom.

A joint approach to managing behaviour

These rewards and sanctions should be applied by all adults:

....

....

....

....

These rewards and sanctions are the responsibility of the lead teacher:

....

....

....

....

What happens if one of us makes a mistake when applying the plan?

....

....

....

....

Which specific students will each of us be monitoring?

....

....

....

....

The agreed procedure for sharing information on behaviour issues in the classroom is:

....

....

....

....

The following students respond particularly well to positive reinforcement, praise and reward:

....

....

....

....

What roles do each of us take in a critical incident?

....

....

....

....

Key ideas summary

Key idea	Benefit for the LSA	Benefit for the students
Meet and plan with the class teacher before you join their class.	The teacher can make informed decisions on how to utilise your skills and dovetail them with her own. The adults can decide how to manage behaviour together.	The students know there is a consistent approach in the classroom from all adults.
Invest time in training yourself and collaborating with the class teacher.	The teacher can share knowledge of strategies that work and how to employ them effectively. The LSA develops their skills in managing behaviour as part of a team and independently.	Students are managed by increasingly skilled, calm and subtle interventions by the support teacher.
All adults work within the agreed framework for behaviour management.	The adults maintain consistency in behaviour management; the rules apply regardless of whom students are working with.	Students are not able to exploit perceived or real differences in rules and expectations between adults.
All adults have responsibility for delivering rewards and sanctions.	The LSA is empowered and encouraged to use positive behaviour management strategies.	Students know that there are positive outcomes for following the directions of the support teacher.
An adult assigned to work with an individual is not precluded from helping others.	The teacher and LSA are able to use some professional judgement in distribution of additional support.	Students are able to approach the LSA for help. The focus student is given some space to breathe, think and make mistakes.

Plan it, write it, do it

Choose a strategy from this chapter to try out. Be realistic about your timescale for implementation and review. It takes at least 30 days to change a habit. Set the criteria by which you will measure the success of the strategy with precision.

Strategy	Resources	Start date	How I will monitor progress	Review date	Success criteria

There is a printable version of the Action Plan on the CD-ROM.

Chapter 13

Involving Parents

'I didn't have any concept of age or authority. I remember realising, Oh, the world has rules and we don't.'

Moon Unit Zappa (daughter of Frank Zappa)

The principle

Parents have a responsibility to support the education of their children and work in partnership with the school. There is a great deal that the school can learn from the parents and vice versa. The teaching team need to nurture and encourage communication with parents who renege on these responsibilities. If contact with parents is always about negative aspects of the child's behaviour, support will ebb away. The more parents can understand the behaviour management frameworks and strategies used in the classroom, the easier it is to communicate accurately with them. As a LSA you have a unique insight into how a student responds to the frustrations of learning. You have vital information that must be shared, either directly or indirectly, with the parents.

The practice

The old metaphor of the child as a three-legged stool supported by school, home and community is still relevant today. Parents are responsible for managing the behaviour of their children, but this is shared with the school and the people who interact with the child in the community. Parents who don't engage in their child's education do so for a reason. They have made a conscious decision to separate school and home. There are many reasons why this happens: the parents' own negative experience of school, overwhelmed with work, not knowing how to become more involved, lack of under-standing about the role of the parent in education, exasperation at their child's behav-iour, anger at the school for some past miscommunication, etc. Regardless of the perceived commitment of the parent you have a responsibility to communicate your expectations clearly. Proactively engaging support from parents/carers is in your own best interests and in the best interests of the student. The additional benefit is that many parents looking for help and advice on how to manage behaviour in the home may adapt ideas that are being used in the classroom.

You may choose to write to parents of the students you work with on a one-to-one basis to inform them of the rules, rewards and sanctions that operate between you and to explain a few of the behaviour management strategies that you are using. Thereafter your communication can take many forms: positive notes home, parents' evenings, positive phone calls home, report cards to be countersigned, impositions (extra work to be completed at home and delivered the following morning) to be checked, phone calls asking for support, text messages, emails. Try to make sure there is some balance between your communications. When you ask for additional support and input because of a period of inappropriate behaviour make sure that parents are also informed when the student's behaviour improves. For students who are persistently disruptive you will need to sow the seeds of a longer-term relationship with the parent(s), remembering that you are unlikely to be the only professional that the parents need to find time for. Try asking for advice and support rather than telling parents what you want them to do. Even if they have no immediate solutions it will open up a dialogue and make it clear that you wish to work in partnership.

You will find that starting communication with parents with positive news about the behaviour of their child is a much easier way in. It also makes them more disposed to support you when there are problems. Make sure that you have triggers built into your strategy that demand personal contact with parents: a series of positive refer-rals might demand a phone call home, just as a series of disruptive lessons might. If you contact parents too late they may question why they were not informed earlier and be shocked at the list of misdemeanours they now need to deal with.

Make sure that you are aware of any child protection issues before you rush to contact home to report bad news about a student. In a small minority of homes a negative communication from school can result in an overreaction that leads to physical punishment. If you know this to be the case, seek advice from a colleague as the connection that the student makes between your contact and corporal punishment may be one that does more harm than good. If you hold a face-to-face meeting with parents do so with a colleague present.

If you are going to communicate effectively with home you will need up-to-date contact information from parents. At the same time it is useful to ask how they would prefer to be contacted. When you are communicating bad news, consider that letters can be intercepted, phone messages can be erased, etc. Try to find the most secure and immediate method of communication that removes responsibility from the student and guarantees that you not only get a message to the child's home, but receive one back. You may choose to use a separate school email address or call a mobile number at an agreed time. Think carefully about the timing of your communication, it may well affect the way in which the information is received and acted upon. You may choose to make contact initially simply to organise a better time to speak at length. This guarantees that the parent will be prepared for the conversation and reserve time to have it.

When there is a bond between home and school the student will see that their behaviour and its consequences are not confined to the classroom. The relationships that you build up with parents are one of the most effective behaviour management levers you can draw on. I would often phone home before the student arrived there or on some memorable occasions be sitting drinking tea with the parent when the student arrived home from school. Once the child knows that a positive relationship exists and that consistent and regular contact is maintained they will check their behaviour carefully and modify responses accordingly.

Most students prefer to separate their home life from their life in school. They are often keen to avoid direct discussion between parents and school representatives. I remember as a student the anxiety the build-up to parents' evenings elicited. Knowing that all of my sins would be laid bare and I would have to confront them in front of my teachers and parents was not a comfortable experience. Try to establish an individual rapport with parents so they know who they are dealing with, they can put a face to a name and over time build up trust in you.

Strategy spotlight

Working on a partnership approach

Find *regular* opportunities to communicate with parents about the child's progress. Don't wait for the parent to come to you at parents' evenings but go over and introduce yourself. Give regular feedback if a student is on subject report, send a note home, or pick up the phone: 'Just giving you a quick call to let you know how Joshua is getting on. . . .'

When you meet parents to discuss their child don't launch straight into the discussion that you really want to have. Often both parties come to the meeting with some apprehension and frustration that needs to be diffused to allow each to relax and share concerns calmly. It is your responsibility to make sure that the meeting goes well and that there is a positive outcome. Avoid discussion about the weather and obvious 'small talk'. Instead try asking after the family, talk about their recent house move or older siblings' progress at university. Show genuine interest in their lives and reinforce your role as a caring professional who is working in the best interests of their child. This will put the parent(s) at ease and you may learn something new that informs your work with the student. Try to connect your concerns about the student's behaviour with your care for their learning and ask for advice on 'what works well at home'. Focus on a partnership approach and look for ways of quickly and efficiently connecting rewards and sanctions at school with those at home.

Watch out for . . .

✔ Becoming too familiar and informal with parents – certainly in the early stages of the relationship they may interpret your throwaway remarks as an indicator of your professionalism and commitment to their child. Keep your conversation friendly but always professional and don't take risks by being indiscreet or flippant.

✔ Making assumptions about the domestic circumstances of a student. Your complaints about the lack of homework may seem trivial when you discover just how many people are living in one house or that there has been a recent bereavement in the family.

✔ 'Telling' parents how to manage the behaviour of their child. Ask for their advice, share some things that seem to be working in the classroom and search for a dialogue that involves everyone in finding strategies that work.

Reflecting on practice

Meet the parent

As a new teacher I was wary of parents. My own lack of understanding about parenting and limited teaching experience made me apprehensive. Tales of parents assaulting staff and trashing the headteacher's office made me think they were best left alone. After all, I wasn't a social worker and I didn't need to know the parents to teach their children.

Damien's roaring, yes roaring, was becoming a real problem. It was loud and persistent and timed for maximum impact in the quiet of the classroom jungle. He had reached the end of every sanction list, class report, school report, broken every classroom rule and had now decided that roaring was the way to go. Talking to the head of year, I asked about what sort of home life Damien had and what impact it might be having on his behaviour. I knew that she had close contact with his parents who were difficult, but she was an extremely skilled operator. 'Come and see,' was her reply. I was not convinced it was a good idea, but I figured that I would be fairly safe with her leading. This would be my first home visit and colleagues gently advised me that it was a road to nowhere.

Damien's house was on a large estate, rundown, sprawling, shops behind steel shutters, burnt out cars, etc. Not somewhere that anyone would choose to live. I had driven around the estate after I had accepted the post, making a mental note to do things the other way around next time, and this was the first time I had seen the houses at close quarters. Walking into the living room I was struck by the smell of dogs (there were five large ones), the noise of the younger children (there were four of them) and the sight of the sofa overflowing with clothes, food, rubbish, etc. In an instant I had a better understanding of Damien. In one moment I realised that his behaviour had more meaning, and even if I couldn't work out the psychology of it, I knew that there was a connection with his home life. His mother apologised profusely, but she was on her own and she could no longer control his behaviour. I explained the problems, she offered sympathy. Damien arrived back from collecting his six-year-old sister from school and the three of us tried to agree a way forward for the next week. He was not a malicious child and in fact could be quite funny, and the atmosphere was quite relaxed. I observed him playing with his younger brothers and sister and taking a great deal of pleasure from it. I saw a gentleness and kindness that was absent from his public persona.

→

I came away from the meeting much better educated about Damien, his home, the parallel homes of other students, the community and the desperation of some parents. I no longer trotted out the line about not being a social worker, learned to be much slower in my judgement of students and began to look further than just the behaviour. My relationship with Damien was deepened: after all, out of all the teachers in the school, there was only the head of year and myself who had seen the other side of his world. Our eye contact had more meaning and although the journey was going to be a long one I knew that it would be easier than before. When colleagues complained that, 'He might be all right in your lesson but he's now squawking and perching on the chair like a bird in mine,' I wanted to tell them why, but they would just call it social work. For me the extra investment of time was paying dividends, my classes could get back to learning and Damien was slowly engaging in the lessons.

I later used the home visit to great effect, shooting round to number 37 straight after school. There I would be eating samosas, discussing Cat Stevens and Asif's behaviour as Asif walked in the door from school. I always took much enjoyment out of watching his face drop as he realised that school and home were no longer separate.

Exercise

Use the pro forma below to draft a letter to all parents informing them about the rules, rewards and sanctions that operate. The letter will seek support and advice, open up a dialogue with home and prepare parents/guardians for your future communications:

Letter pro forma

Dear Parent/Guardian,

I would like to keep you up to date with some of the behaviour management strategies that I am using with your child/a small group of students. If you have any advice on the strategies that work well for your child I would appreciate the feedback.

There are .... *(insert number)* rules that operate when we are working together:

Rules

....
....
....
....

When students follow the rules they are rewarded using the following steps:

Rewards

....
....
....
....

If students choose not to follow the rules they can expect the following stepped sanctions:

Sanctions

....
....
....

I have adopted this framework to make the learning positive, consistent and safe. Students have been reminded that the following behaviours fall outside of the stepped sanctions and will result in .... *(insert high-level sanction).*

Extreme behaviour

(Violent, racist or aggressive behaviour, swearing at the teacher, etc.)

....

I aim to communicate with you as soon as possible when students reach high-level sanctions or repeatedly make poor choices. I will also make sure that I inform you when your child is behaving well. You can expect me to:

....

(Send positive notes home, call you/text/email when students are doing well – do keep me updated with changes in contact information), let you know if your child starts making poor choices, be consistent and fair in my application of the rules, ask for advice when I need it.)

If you could discuss this plan with your child at home it would really help them start to see that we are working together to help them succeed.

Yours truly,

....

Key ideas summary

Key idea	Benefit for the LSA	Benefit for the students
Proactively nurturing and engaging support from parents.	By working in partnership you are making a clear connection between home and school for the student. You are able to call on support and advice when necessary.	Students are supported with increasing consistency, they are surrounded by agreed expectations.
Communicate with home regularly, with positive news and for seeking support. Let students know that you are communicating directly.	If the teaching staff are communicating regularly with positive feedback it is easier to elicit support when needed.	Students know there is a direct link between the classroom and home. They use this knowledge when deciding whether to disrupt.
Ask for advice and support from parents rather than simply telling them what you want them to do.	The LSA can learn from the experiences at home. Parents will be more willing to listen if they have been listened to first.	As ideas are shared the partnership between home and school is developed; joint strategies for managing certain behaviours are agreed.
Check with an appropriate colleague before contacting home with bad news.	The LSA avoids prompting an unwanted reaction from home and is prepared for any hostility.	Vulnerable students are protected as information is communicated carefully and sensitively.
Ask parents how and when they prefer to be contacted.	The conversation is not rushed and there is more time to choose your words with care.	Students are not involved in running messages between home and school that can easily go astray.

Plan it, write it, do it

Choose a strategy from this chapter to try out. Be realistic about your timescale for implementation and review. It takes at least 30 days to change a habit. Set the criteria by which you will measure the success of the strategy with precision.

Strategy	Resources	Start date	How I will monitor progress	Review date	Success criteria

There is a printable version of the Action Plan on the CD-ROM.

PART 4

Specific Situations

Chapter 14

Managing Extreme Behaviour

'Hey Joe, where you going with that gun in your hand?'

Jimi Hendrix

The principle

Every child matters, even the disruptive ones. Some of the students you work with will have a complicated history and patterns of negative behaviour that are destructive, disruptive and designed to make most adults throw their hands up in despair and run away. You are responsible for managing the behaviour of the students you work with regardless of their individual needs. Even students with the most extreme emotional and behavioural difficulties can and do succeed with the right support. Applying the rules and rewards will need considered professional judgement and you may need to adapt the hierarchy in order to meet the needs of the individual. To have a chance of succeeding with students who experience difficulty in controlling their behaviour you will need to invest time in your relationship with them and accept that this investment is for the long term. Students with behavioural difficulties can have years of learned behaviour to unravel before they start to turn the corner. You need to be patient, kind and determined not to give up on any of your students. You are the adult and you need to keep a clear perspective even when these students reject your kindness and empathy.

The practice

It would be very easy to declare that everyone, regardless of their individual needs, must follow the same rules when they are working with you. Working with students with behavioural difficulties is not that linear or rigid. It requires a more flexible approach. Everybody needs to accept that at different times you will make decisions that may not appear fair but are in the best interests of individuals. Differentiating your management of behaviour is akin to differentiating the work that students are doing. If we expected the same standard of work from each student we would soon be disillusioned. The same can be said of behaviour. It is right and fair to differentiate the way we deal with the behaviour of individuals who haven't learned how to, or who don't want to, play our game.

Very often EBD students – those with emotional and behavioural difficulties – will be working with a team of people in the school and those from external frontline support services. There may be many different people negotiating or setting behaviour targets: parents, the form tutor, senior member of staff, specialist behaviour teacher, social worker, probation officer, counsellor, etc. With everyone working in the best interests of the child the support provided ought to have an impact over the medium and long term. In the short term and at the class level it is very difficult for professionals who are not present to have an immediate impact on behaviour.

Every Child Matters

Every Child Matters: Change for Children in Schools (DfES, 2004) sets out clear expectations and guidelines for information sharing and collaboration between agencies for implementation by 2008. Its focus on 'extended services' promises to deliver study support, family learning, parental support opportunities and better referral to multi-agency support. For students who need to be removed from mainstream education on a temporary or permanent basis, the work of pupil referral units is given prominence. The work of education welfare officers (EWOs) is supported by truancy sweeps, and a range of measures designed to catch those students who fall off the education radar. There is certainly a great backlog to catch up on with many students who have been permanently excluded and still have no formal access to education. If the delivery of *Every Child Matters* matches the rhetoric it will help those families and students in most need to find successful routes to learning that are more focused on the individual.

Senior colleagues who have a high level of input with a challenging student will often encounter them, report card in hand, being escorted down the corridor after engaging in precisely the behaviours they have spent two days discussing. Colleagues are distraught as it seems that even the middle management and external agencies are having no impact. For students who have difficulty managing their behaviour the process of change can be slow and frustrating for everyone concerned. With your unique perspective on the day-to-day responses of the student you can provide relevant information, collaborate with others and encourage change.

At a class level the visible impact of additional support may be the student waving their report card in your face. The report will have pre-agreed targets, rules and (for some students) procedures to follow for removing them from the lesson.

Don't be tempted to undermine the work of others by doing any of the following:

✘ Using the report as a negotiating tool with the student to try and bribe them into behaving appropriately: 'If you stop hitting Clive I will give you a good report.'

✘ Allow the student to negotiate their way into a good report after a lesson where they didn't follow the rules or achieve their targets: 'Aw go on, sir, give me a tick for that one, I was really good this lesson. Please sir, Arsenal won, you must be in a good mood.' (They are very good at it and know that it works.)

✘ Try to avoid confrontation with the student by giving them a good report. There are some students who will fly into a rage or descend into tears when they see what you have recorded on their reports. Their reaction, however extreme, should not influence your judgement on whether they have met their targets.

✘ Write anything on the report that is a judgement on the student: 'Still can't behave, rude boy.'

✘ Leave reports where they can be read/taken by other students.

In some circumstances it is preferable to return the report card to the student at the door, on their way out of the lesson, having filled it in already. This can help to avoid confrontation as the student reads the outcome. The reason that report cards can be such a flashpoint is that the student has sanctions hanging over them that they would much rather avoid. They may have sanctions linked between home and school that affect their social time, access to media, income, etc. The fact that they are worried about their sanctions is a good thing and might just be enough to move some students away from the edge. By fulfilling your responsibilities at the class level you are making it clear to the student that their destiny is in their own hands. Try:

✔ Reinforcing the ritual for the report card to be given to you rather than thrown on the desk.

✔ Giving sincere praise and encouragement for students who follow the rules and achieve targets.

✔ Showing concern if you see from the card that the student is having a bad day.

✔ Reminding students on report that every good lesson stands out and counts in their favour (even if the previous four lessons have gone very badly).

✔ Making time for students, be it in tutor/form group, lunchtime or at an appropriate time in the lesson, for those who are keen to show and discuss their report with you.

Although I recognise that report card systems are not a universal solution and only deal with the symptoms they do provide valuable information for monitoring behaviour across the curriculum, providing a framework for discussion and targeting intervention. Many students find the process allows them a chance to reflect on their behaviour. Some will ask to be 'put on report', others will use the report card blank to evaluate their own behaviour and then discuss the results at the end of the day/week with their form teacher.

You are able to instigate an 'LSA report' to monitor the behaviour of individuals who are causing concern. You may chose to do this in collaboration with the class teacher or instigate it on your own. This can be particularly useful when monitoring students who display sequences of inappropriate behaviour when they work with you. The fact that the report is sent up the internal chain and also sent home gives it weight. You will often find that it only takes a few bad lessons for the student to realise that a sheet of paper with incidents recorded and dated is not going to go down well with its intended audience. Typically students strive to improve their choices to balance the initially negative behaviour. Your regular conversations with the student will also give you the opportunity to focus on positive changes and reinforce them strongly. Use the template on the CD-ROM to design your own 'class report' form.

'I can't teach this child; it's not fair on the rest of the class'

We have all heard this and sometimes more than once, but it is worth considering what happens when we give up on a student and begin the process of excluding them from education. I know we enter a wider political realm here, but it starts in individual class-rooms and escalates from there.

The situation is not uncommon. The behaviour of an individual pupil is extreme and disruptive to the rest of the learning. Their needs appear to be so complex you begin to question why they are not accommodated elsewhere. You have tried and failed to manage their behaviour successfully, and you have watched as colleagues have tried to intervene and provide support, but appear to be making little impact. Exasperated, you demand that the student is excluded from the class/refused additional support. They are duly removed; you breathe a heavy sigh of relief and feel that your actions are in the best interests of the majority of the students. For the short term, they may be.

A student who is repeatedly excluded is likely to be in a cycle of negative behaviour:

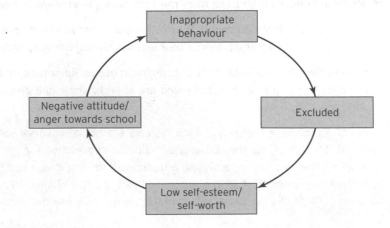

By excluding the student we allow the cycle to continue. There are certainly a small minority of students who cannot fit into mainstream or special education and it is right that they should be given opportunities to be educated elsewhere. There are a more significant number who are simply moved around from class to class and school to school. These students learn fairly quickly that adults cannot always be relied on to support them. Many students with emotional and behavioural difficulties know this already from home. Adults who have shown commitment to them in the past can leave suddenly. In school their distrust of adults is reconfirmed by adults who give up on them. The message they can infer from both sides is that there is something wrong with them.

Don't give up on any individual and tell them so. You may need to exclude students as part of higher-level sanctions but this should always be temporary and you will need to commit time outside of the classroom to providing additional support: phone and visit parents; stay after school; arrange for extra support in lessons and from outside agencies; and be proactive in developing a trusting relationship with the student.

Successful LSAs go the extra mile, not just because they care about the individual who is experiencing difficulties but also because of the rest of the class. They send a clear message that their job is to ensure everyone succeeds and that as a class everyone has a responsibility to support each other. In the classroom, as in life, there will be people who at different times find it hard to fit in. Rather than rejecting these people we need to show them care, compassion and respect. Part of your role is to model this, demonstrating to your students an inclusive approach to learning together.

There will be times when many of the students in a group will need additional support in managing their behaviour. Your sole focus cannot always be the majority of students. In that majority there are students who may not need extra attention today but will do tomorrow. Aim to try and break or at least slow down the cycles of negative behaviour. Saying: 'I can't teach this child,' says more about your commitment to your students than it does about behaviour that is difficult to manage.

Checklist on the steps you have taken to remedy the behaviour of the student

✔ Adapted, individualised and negotiated rules, rewards and sanctions applied.

✔ Short-term targets that are reinforced by praise, acknowledgement and reward have been set.

✔ Consistently and calmly applied sanctions.

✔ Kept a detailed record of behaviour over the course of eight lessons.

✔ Initiated face-to-face discussion with parents and obtained the support of senior staff.

✔ Drawn up a behaviour contract/agreement with everyone concerned having an input (see the CD-ROM).

✔ Agreed a mechanism with the student to indicate when they need 'time out' (see the CD-ROM).

✔ Adjusted seating plan.

✔ Agreed strategies with other adults working in the classroom.

✔ Kept praise, reward and sanctions discreet and private.

✔ Used modelling to reflect behaviour back to the student and help them to gain a better perspective on their actions.

✔ Sought guidance from senior or key colleague.

✔ Referred to appropriate internal channels and chased these referrals.

✔ Provided information and support to encourage the input of external agencies.

✔ Gone out of your way to invest time and energy into building a relationship with the student.

✔ Considered carefully whether the student is part of a small minority who need specialist schooling or whether they are part of the larger group of students that can be included in mainstream education.

Your targets for students who struggle to stay within acceptable boundaries need to be short-term. Providing a target for the end of the next lesson may be appropriate for students who are in control of their behaviour, but for EBD students it may be necessary to set a target for the next five minutes of work. You will also need to explain your expectations and targets for their social conduct alongside this. Do not assume that they know how to work in groups or even individually. If you are trying to break a negative pattern of behaviour it is important that your starting point is that EBD students do not know how to behave appropriately. Just as early years teachers know it is their responsibility to teach the children social skills and strategies, so with EBD students you must build this into your daily routine.

Match your short-term targets with short-term praise and rewards that can be agreed with the student. It is important to realise that students with an EBD label don't often attract regular praise and rewards. They are more likely to be closely observed for inappropriate behaviour and you need to change this focus. I'm not suggesting that you heap rewards on challenging students. It is your verbal praise and acknowledgement that is most important. If you set a five-minute target, and the student reaches this, or makes strong moves towards it, then it must be immediately reinforced if the level of work is to be sustained. Do it privately and discreetly. Use eye contact, non-verbal cues and written comments to let the student know that their behaviour is appreciated and valued. Be prepared for your responses to be rejected and even thrown back in your face. If you really want to break the cycle, it will take patience and commitment. Nurture a relationship where students are expected to succeed, where you are utterly consistent, and the seeds of trust will be allowed to grow.

When incidents occur, and they will, your response to them is crucial. Many students with a history of negative behaviour have learnt that extreme behaviour results in dramatic responses from adults. They may have slipped into negative behaviour patterns because they enjoy these reactions. If you want to break the cycle, your responses should be carefully measured, even in the most challenging situations. With your emotional brain carefully in check, and verbal and physical language controlled, calmly go through the same script. You may find it useful to use the exemplar scripts or the sample structure for intervention (in Chapter 7).

Using a 'time out' card

Some students have difficulty in controlling their anger and/or frustration, but can recognise when they are about to lose it. With these students you may find it useful to use a 'time out' card. The card is held by the student and placed on the desk when they need to leave the room to calm down. You will need to set a limit to the amount of times the student can use this in a single lesson. With some students it may be necessary to connect the use of the card with the requirement to complete a think sheet (see the CD-ROM) to allow them to reflect on what brought them to this point. This will encourage students not to overuse the card and allow you to reflect with them and plan for the next lesson.

Being proactive means that you need to find time for the student outside the classroom. Make a point of talking to them around the school and in social areas. Seek them out to talk to. Just one or two minutes of conversation a day can slowly open the door to a positive professional relationship.

Let colleagues, parents and external agencies know when that student decides to follow the rules. Record your comments on paper as verbal feedback can be lost. There will inevitably be detailed documentation on their crimes and misdemeanours; you have a responsibility to record their positive behaviour with as much care.

Modelling and 'holding up the mirror'

A colleague and friend tells of a student who responded to even the simplest request with the exaggerated grunts, sighs and flinches that we most associate now with Harry Enfield's or Catherine Tate's teenage characters. She became exasperated with his behaviour and decided to tackle it head-on.

Holding the student behind during the lunch hour, and in private, she sought the support of a colleague and asked the student if he minded watching while she demonstrated the behaviour that she was observing from him. He agreed and she mimicked, fairly accurately, a typical response to a straightforward request: 'Could I have a look at your work, please?', 'What! (sighs), oh God (exhales loudly, tutting, more sighing, etc.), get out of my face, etc.' At the end of her demonstration the boy was ashen-faced. He was shocked at the reflection of his own behaviour and felt embarrassed that other students had seen him behave in this way. In an instant he resolved to check his behaviour with more care.

Many of us would assume that he was aware of his original behaviour pattern and engaging in it deliberately. It was the clarity of the teacher's judgement and her careful and sensitive use of modelling that turned the situation round. She was able to hold up the mirror to his behaviour and allow him to accept this information in a controlled environment.

Younger students need this mirror as they find it difficult to externalise their own behaviour. The six-year-old who pleads repeatedly to be allowed to go first only sees the situation from his own viewpoint. Encouraging him to see his behaviour from the outside allows him to begin understanding the impact it has on others.

Watch out for . . .

✔ Making assumptions about a student's behaviour because of their label or from what you have heard about them in the staffroom. EBD students rarely get the opportunity to have a clean sheet and can feel the weight of their label/reputation pulling them into a negative pattern. There is nothing more soul-destroying for a student who is trying to find a way of changing people's attitudes towards them, to find that new people they meet have already made up their minds.

✔ Getting frustrated because the student does not appear to be modifying their disruptive behaviour patterns. Regardless of your level of skill, you are not going to turn them round in an instant. Set your targets for improving their behaviour in the longer term: think about months and years, instead of days and weeks.

✔ Contacting home without first checking with the appropriate member of staff. It is likely that the school will already have identified the most effective communication with home. This may be carefully planned and regular. Picking up the phone or making unauthorised contact may trample on the work of other professionals. You also need to think about what the consequences for the student may be at home. There may be very good reasons why senior staff are the primary point of contact within the school.

✔ Assuming inappropriate behaviour is directed at you. The student who swears in frustration because he doesn't understand how to engage in the work is not swearing directly at you. Although you may not agree with the student's choice of language or choice of behaviour, you need to accept that their reactions may not be the same as other students'. Whilst you should not ignore inappropriate behaviour, measure and differentiate your response.

Issues to consider

There are a number of issues that LSAs have no direct influence on, but which affect the management of behaviour. Students who have been diagnosed with ADHD (attention-deficit hyperactivity disorder) or other emotional or behavioural disorders, students prescribed behaviour modification drugs, students who are malnourished, exhausted through lack of sleep, experimenting with controlled drugs or troubled by a complicated domestic situation present themselves in the classroom and their behaviour needs to be managed. It is important that you are as informed as possible about the external factors that directly impact on behaviour in the classroom. Your knowledge and understanding of the key issues may be useful when you are asked for advice by parents and you will be able to take best advantage of opportunities to have a positive influence.

ADHD

There is much conflicting evidence about ADHD. Critics argue that it is a convenient label that gives a medical reason for poor behaviour; others point to the use of brain-imaging techniques that demonstrates that it has a biological basis. ADHD, which is also known as attention-deficit disorder (or ADD), hyperkinetic child syndrome, minimal brain damage, minimal brain dysfunction in children, minimal cerebral dysfunction and psycho-organic syndrome in children, is a remarkably non-specific disorder. The symptoms that characterise the disorder may include a chronic history of a short attention span, distractibility, impulsivity and moderate to severe hyperactivity. Learning may or may not be impaired.

There is certainly little consistency in diagnosis, and moving between schools it is not unusual to find students with the same label demonstrating few similar symptoms or even similar behaviours. The truth is that some parents will push for a diagnosis of ADHD in search of a reason for a temporary period of poor behaviour, and some over-worked doctors will submit to this too easily. However, this does not negate the accurate and extremely worrying diagnosis for students who genuinely have a long-term medical condition. The treatment for ADHD will, in part, necessitate a behavioural approach with home, school and external support agencies working in partnership. Some of the symptoms of ADHD can be masked by the use of prescription drugs and you will work with students who ride that rollercoaster every day.

Practical strategies for ADHD

✔ Confronting the student's negative internal monologue with praise, positive reinforcement and carefully chosen language.

✔ Adapting, individualising, negotiating and contracting rules, rewards and sanctions.

✔ Setting/agreeing short-term targets.

✔ 'Chunking' tasks into shorter pieces.

✔ Softening the impact of high-level sanctions by providing a positive model of the student's previous good behaviour.

✔ Recording and monitoring patterns of behaviour.

✔ Adjusting the seating plan to find the best configuration for the student.

✔ Using modelling to reflect back to the student how their behaviour is viewed by those looking on

✔ Allowing and encouraging more active approaches to learning.

✔ Allowing the student to take regular breaks from the desk and table.

✔ Reinforcing the rules and rituals before beginning an activity.

✔ Reducing formal talk time.

Prescription drugs

When a child has been given a medical label it is possible to offer a treatment. The amphetamine-based drug Ritalin is widely used to counter the behavioural symptoms of ADHD and its use is extremely controversial.

In the US, doctors write 2 million prescriptions for ADHD drugs for children every month and 1 million for adults. In the UK behaviour modification drugs are licensed for children as young as six (although there are reports of them being given to children as young as three). In Scotland prescriptions for drugs relating to ADHD have risen by over 20% in one year (Scotland's Information Services Division, January 2008). Michael Schlander of the University of Heidelberg in Germany created a model based on demographic and epidemiological data, past spending trends, and an assessment of which drugs may soon be available for prescriptions. He calculated a range of the possible costs by varying the assumptions made for factors such as the likelihood of diagnosis and treatment, the level of treatment and the cost of drugs. The cost of ADHD prescriptions to the NHS in England was £7 million in 2002 and the study predicted that this will rise to somewhere between £49 and £101 million per year by 2012. Prof Schlander stated: "The scenarios developed here strongly suggest that the trend of rising drug expenditures for ADHD may not abate in the near future."

These figures are shocking and probably don't reflect the true number of students taking medication. If you could include parents who are bypassing their GP and buying them on the Internet, 'without prescription, by credit card, by overnight courier', the figures are bound to rise. Figures from the Prescriptions Pricing Authority reveal that there has been a 180-fold increase in prescriptions since 1991 when only 2,000 were issued in England.

Children as young as six, whose brains are still developing, are being prescribed mind-altering drugs. In America there are documented cases of children as young as 15 months being prescribed Ritalin. Yet many doctors are concerned that Ritalin is being wrongly prescribed and used as a sticking plaster for a period of poor behaviour

'Ritalin does not correct biochemical imbalances – it causes them.'
(Peter R. Breggin MD, Director of the International Center for the Study of Psychiatry and Psychology and associate faculty member at Johns Hopkins University)

A child taking Ritalin might have more focused behaviour. But although that might mean less disruption in the classroom, does it really help the child? And should we give a child a powerful and potentially hazardous drug because it keeps him quiet? So many unanswered questions remain: What about the growing evidence that problems can be stored up for later for students on medication? Is it morally excusable to give drugs to young children that have no long-term benefits for them?

When children are prescribed strong medication it must be a cause of grave concern to everyone; when it is on this scale the search for preventative and alternative treatment takes on an increased urgency.

Nutrition

There are alternatives to quick-fix drugs for students who are diagnosed with or demonstrate symptoms of ADHD. The evidence of a link between nutrition and behaviour is compelling. We have always been able to recognise students who arrive at school without a proper breakfast. From slipping a hungry child an apple, to free milk and breakfast clubs, to the removal of sugar-laden vending machines, schools know student behaviour and achievement are linked to food. With behavioural disorders there is a more urgent need to educate parents and children about the benefits of foods that effect a low release of energy throughout the day rather than a short burst of sugar that results in a 'crash' shortly afterwards.

For students with behavioural disorders there is strong evidence that nutrition can treat not just the symptom but also the root cause.

The benefits of fish oils

Alexandra Richardson studied more than 100 children of normal ability in mainstream schools in County Durham who were underachieving and suspected of being dyspraxic – that is, of having problems with coordination or motor skills. In some cases, the children were also disruptive.

Once they had been assessed, they were divided into two groups for a randomised double-blind, placebo-controlled trial. Half of them were given fish oils high in Omega-3 essential fats for three months. The other half were given placebos. Some 40 per cent of the children given supplements made dramatic improvements in reading and spelling, averaging progress of more than nine months in just three months. The control group made just the normal progress of three months.

Although none had been diagnosed as suffering from ADHD, a third were found to have sufficient problems to put them in this category. But when given fish oils, half of them made so much progress they no longer counted as having attention disorders – a change on a par with improvements made when children are prescribed stimulant drugs such as Ritalin.

Asperger's syndrome and autism–Autistic Spectrum Disorders (ASD)

Asperger's syndrome is variant of autism. Young people with Asperger's present different individual variations of the condition. No two people with the condition are the same. Although this guidance may help you to understand some of the key issues and practical strategies you will need to get to know the student well and adapt ideas accordingly.

Asperger's is predominantly a male condition (9:1 male:female). Lorna Wing (Burgoine and Wing, 1983) describe the main clinical features of Asperger's syndrome:

- lack of empathy;
- naïve, inappropriate, one-sided interaction;
- little or no ability to form friendships;
- pedantic, repetitive speech;
- poor non-verbal communication;
- intense absorption in certain subjects;
- clumsy and ill-coordinated movements and odd postures.

Those who are diagnosed with Asperger's syndrome, autism, ASD, and to some extent ADHD, view or interpret the world very differently. As a teacher you need to understand how their condition affects their perception. There are practical strategies you can adopt, but these must be adjusted for the individual, implemented with empathy and have the flexibility to be adapted for different contexts. The strategies that you use for managing the behaviour of other students are still relevant here with certain aspects given more emphasis;

- Consistency and predictability – of lesson structure, intervention, response.

- The adult's emotional control: don't take it personally even if the student appears to be rude – 'You are fat' – their frankness may be result of their literal world.

- Planned and controlled use of language (verbal, tonal and physical), avoiding sarcasm, over-exaggeration and imagery. Communication should be precise as it may be interpreted literally: 'I am going to explode!' may mean exactly that to the autistic student.

- Modelling appropriate behaviour and basic routines/rules. Model for and with other students to show those with the condition how to communicate effectively. Model for the student with the condition to show them precisely the behaviours that you want.

- Encourage positive friendships and help the student to make and sustain positive relationships with others.

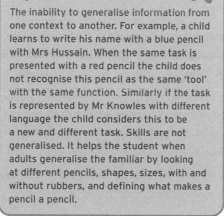

Key feature of autism

The inability to generalise information from one context to another. For example, a child learns to write his name with a blue pencil with Mrs Hussain. When the same task is presented with a red pencil the child does not recognise this pencil as the same 'tool' with the same function. Similarly if the task is represented by Mr Knowles with different language the child considers this to be a new and different task. Skills are not generalised. It helps the student when adults generalise the familiar by looking at different pencils, shapes, sizes, with and without rubbers, and defining what makes a pencil a pencil.

- Time out to release tension – accepting that at times the control they exert over their behaviour may have built up tension that needs to be released.

- Routines, rules and rituals – visual (signs, symbols and language) and consistently applied rituals of praise and sanction.

- Visual cues, visual support for learning.

- Physical environment – size and division of space, level and range of noise (particularly unexpected noise).

- Preparation for changes to the normal routine.

Practical strategies and ideas for Asperger's syndrome and autism

✔ Take care over transitions between activities. Prepare the student for the transition in good time, establishing the rituals for transitions and mapping the transition as a visual routine on the wall.

✔ Help the student to make the connections between object and language by providing alternative questions: e.g 'Please shut the door' may get no response but 'Please close the door' may. Then link the words 'shut' and 'close' with the student.

✔ Have a clear visual plan of the lesson in the same place for the student to look at when they enter. Break the lesson down into chunks and use symbols or photographs so that they know what to expect: e.g. 1. Sitting and listening; 2. Writing; 3. Group discussion, etc.

✔ Explain the sequence of a complex task. You might prepare for the arrival of the student by using the other students to model the routines on video or as a series of photographs.

✔ Apply rewards and consequences calmly using visual cues – tickets/Post-its/pictures.

✔ Make a series of flashcards with clear symbols to show to the student if they are interrupting or shouting out at inappropriate times. Use a keyring to hold the cards and to easily flip from one to the next.

✔ Give the student a 'time out' card that they can leave on your desk if they need to leave the room and release some tension. The card might say: 'I need to leave the room now, I am not being rude, I just need to take 5.' Again this card could be designed with symbols or using a photograph.

✔ Be vigilant of students misinterpreting body language, tone of voice, facial expression, gesture, intent.

✔ Use a picture dictionary to introduce new vocabulary and support learning with concrete materials.

✔ When necessary, reduce your language to key words to emphasise the main message you are trying to convey. When you are delivering instructions try using a similar tone and the same key words each time.

✔ Frequently a student with ASD will be an excellent decoder of language, reading fluently and with ease, and yet may not have comprehended what has been read. Check for understanding, help the student to bridge the gaps in comprehension, give extra time to reread when necessary.

✔ Carefully choose pupils for paired activities and encourage turn taking, sharing responsibility for the task.

✔ Use mind maps to link ideas and timelines to show the passage of time

✔ Use the other students as models for appropriate behaviour. Ask the student to observe the others and copy what they are doing.

✔ Encourage simple cooperative games.

✔ Explain alternative means of seeking help: the student may consider that the teacher is the sole source of information and assistance.

✔ Encourage prospective friendships.

✔ Be aware of two characters. Many students control their behaviour for a period of time and then can keep it up no longer.

✔ Think carefully about activities that involve loud, unexpected attacks on the senses: e.g. loud noises, rowdy groups, bright lights, sudden movement.

Television

LSAs experience the effect of television on children every day. These effects range from seemingly harmless play acting *Power Rangers* in the playground, to changes in language brought about by American 'gangsta' slang, to irritable students suffering from sleep deprivation. There is mounting evidence that watching too much television is changing the way in which children concentrate and learn.

'[Television] stunts the development of children's brains, increases the likelihood of children developing ADHD and may permanently hinder children's educational progress.'

(Dr Aric Sigman, *Remotely Controlled*)

In particular, television has been shown to have a particularly detrimental effect on younger children, damaging and changing the nature and span of attention. Like fastfood that has been developed to keep people eating, television has developed refined techniques to keep people watching. The most common problem seems to be the proliferation of screens in children's bedrooms. Survey the students you work with and you may be surprised just how many students have got televisions (cable ready with 250 channels), computers and game consoles that they can watch and play in bed. Often without parental control they are able to access programming throughout the night, receiving images that are designed for an adult audience.

There are obvious issues of access to unsuitable materials and associated concerns about students giving time to reading, sleep, outdoor play, having conversations with parents and siblings, being comfortable with silence and developing their own inner voice and thoughts. In many homes the television is the first thing to be switched on in the morning and the last thing to be switched off at night. Even when families leave the house, access to television and new media is unrestricted – in cars, in school cafés, on mobile phones, on aeroplanes, via handheld DVD and hard drives, etc. With the arrival of interactive whiteboards and computer projection some classrooms are beginning to resemble mini lecture theatres. LSAs and students are forced to spend a great deal, if not all, of the lesson, staring at a screen. Both groups, but for different reasons, will have spent most of the previous evening staring at a screen. Is it really benefiting children to create and develop their understanding of the world through a series of media screens? For parents to use television to rear their offspring? For educators to rely solely on digital media to present ideas?

Controlled drugs

If you suspect that students are under the influence of controlled drugs (including alcohol) whilst in school, try to gather evidence rather than jumping in with accusations. Whether you are right or not you are unlikely to improve the situation by publicly declaring your judgement. Deal with the students immediate behaviour professionally whilst subtly seek a second opinion from a colleague. You can then report to and discuss your observations with a senior colleague. A sizeable minority of students will always want to experiment with controlled substances. Your responsibility is to reinforce the policy of no drugs in school, and open clear pathways for students to seek advice and guidance whilst maintaining positive relationships. If experimentation develops into a regular habit it is those with the most developed relationships that are likely to have most influence on the student.

Mobile phones

Some 65 per cent of children aged 8-15 have their own mobile phone; 49 per cent of 8-11-year-olds and 82 per cent of 12-15 year-olds likewise. (Ofcom Media Literacy Audit, October 2006). Mobile phones mean new behaviour challenges for teachers: receiving and making calls in lessons, sending and receiving texts, accessing the Internet, playing games, taking photographs, and recording audio and video are all common activities that students want to pursue in class. Then there are the associated problems of theft, selling and receiving stolen phones and SIM cards, 'happy slapping' videos, malicious bullying via texting and candid photography. At a time when schools are struggling to meet the behavioural needs of students, the advent of the mobile phone in schools has not helped. Some schools have banned mobile phones only to find students covertly using them, and parents undermining the rules by phoning their children in the middle of the day: 'Can you put the phone away, please', 'It's my dad, you'll have to wait a minute!' If we could step away from the fear and paranoia that drives parents to insist on direct and immediate contact with their children (in part perpetuated by the commercial interests of the mobile companies) perhaps the government could allow schools to use signal blockers (widely available but currently illegal in the UK) so that the mobile becomes redundant in the classroom. These devices are cheap, effective and would solve the related challenges in the classroom at a stroke. LSAs could spend more time on their teaching, students could put their social lives on hold while they are learning, and everyone would accept that there is an appropriate time and place for communicating with the outside world.

Phone pickling

An alternative, perhaps light-hearted, strategy was suggested to me to encourage students to leave their phones turned off in their bags. The teacher in question had a large glass jar on top of the filing cabinet in her room containing vinegar and a number of broken mobile phones floating inside. Students new to the group would notice the jar immediately and ask why there were phones in there. The reply was a throw-away line about how some of her previous students had got their phones out in class time and she had yet to throw these away. The students get the message using some humour (no, I am not suggesting anyone actually destroys phones) and it is certainly a much better sign that the usual mobile phone in a red circle with a cross next to it. In this particular class there was no one brave enough to test the idea and phones remain switched off and out of view to this day.

Exercise

Over the course of five lessons use the chart to record the number of positive *interventions* (positive reinforcement, verbal praise, positive non-verbal cues, rewards) against the number of *sanctions* given.

Focus on raising the number of positive interventions lesson by lesson. An example of a filled-in chart is shown below.

Example of a filled-in chart

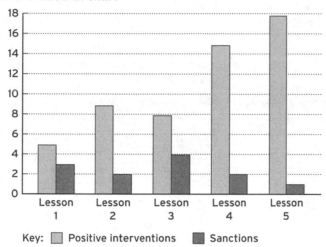

An empty chart to be filled in by the LSA

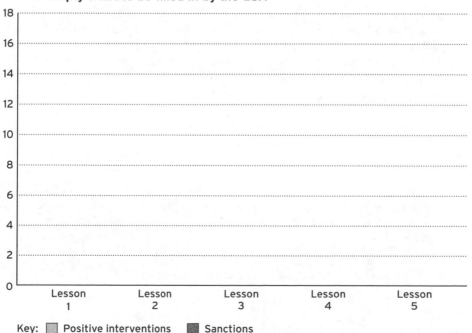

Key ideas summary

Key idea	Benefit for the LSA	Benefit for the student(s)
Being flexible in your design and application of rewards and sanctions.	Allows the LSA to change the frequency and level of intervention to best meet the needs of the individual.	Being part of discussions on rewards and sanctions. The student, whose behaviour is not linear, appreciates the flexibility the LSA is able to allow.
Aiming for success over a longer timescale.	The LSA is able to plan for smaller changes over a longer period of time and avoid the frustration of expecting immediate change.	Gives the student more time to unravel learned negative behaviours.
Using short-term targets.	Target setting is at the task level and the student is closely monitored. Short-term targets encourage sustained periods of appropriate behaviour.	Targets are more immediate and there is less opportunity to drift off task.
Careful consideration of the seating plan.	Students can be positioned so that they are able to support rather than disrupt the learning of their neighbour. Peer groups who spar off each other can be separated.	Students have the opportunity to learn away from their friends and integrate with other students.
Measured responses to inappropriate or extreme behaviour.	Keeps your emotional brain in check and avoids repeated confrontation with students.	Students are able to predict your responses. Their extreme behaviour does not elicit the extreme response that they desire.
Proactively developing a relationship with the student.	Builds trust with the student. Allows for greater understanding of individual needs and circumstances.	Builds trust with the LSA, which can lead to respect. Student begins to listen to and value your opinions. It matters when you are unhappy about their behaviour.
Seeking advice and reporting back to senior colleagues, outside agencies and parents.	The LSA doesn't feel isolated and learns from the other professionals.	The student sees the LSA as part of a team of people working in their best interests. The student is accountable for their behaviour in class to a wider audience.

Plan it, write it, do it

Choose a strategy from this chapter to try out. Be realistic about your timescale for implementation and review. It takes at least 30 days to change a habit. Set the criteria by which you will measure the success of the strategy with precision.

Strategy	Resources	Start date	How I will monitor progress	Review date	Success criteria

There is a printable version of the Action Plan on the CD-ROM.

Chapter 15

Withdrawing a Small Group

'When I look at the smiles on all the children's faces, I just know they're about to jab me with something.'

Homer J Simpson

The principle

When you withdraw a group of students to work elsewhere on the site or cover for the regular teacher you are accountable for the management of the students within your care. You also have a responsibility to the regular teacher to ensure you maintain their expectations and quality of teaching (assuming these match or exceed your own!). Maintaining control in another teacher's classroom environment or in a multi-use area with a different seating plan, unfamiliar students and in a subject in which you may have little confidence, presents its own challenges. Without careful preparation, behaviour management can be more complicated.

The practice

In order to manage the behaviour of students who are not as familiar with your rules, rewards and sanctions you need to work hard throughout the session, but especially at the start. There will inevitably be some students who see a change in teacher or environment as an opportunity to avoid work. The questioning and negotiating begins: 'Do we have to do any work today?', 'Have you got our books because we don't have them?', 'Can we just talk for a bit?', 'Miss normally lets us keep our coats on.' 'Have you got a boyfriend, Miss?', etc. They can sense your apprehension at being alone with the group and away from the regular teacher. For your management of behaviour to be effective you need to be proactive.

Some practical strategies

Start at the door of the room, enthusiastically welcoming the students and catching them doing the right thing. Give them clear instructions about where to put their bags and coats and show them that you are keen to explore the work with them. If you have never met the students before then giving them large sticky labels to write their names on and fix to their clothing is a good idea. It won't necessarily stop all students swapping names, but it will allow you to speak to the majority of students using their first names and more accurately record any incidents. Alternatively you might have prepared a seating plan with name labels on the desks. If you identify difficulties early with the seating plan move students around straight away. It is much easier to move students in the early stages of the session; it causes less disruption to the learning. If you have a group who find it difficult to work at the same table bring them together to explain the task and then move them to individual working areas. Explain to the group that you expect everyone to be working throughout and for this reason you will make changes to seating as necessary. If students complain that you are changing their usual seating plan, explain that you are leading the session, and you get to set the ground rules. You may choose to allow more freedom with the seating plan for students who earn that right by their willingness to follow the rules.

Your physical and verbal language is very important when taking a group of students away from the class. They are watching to see just how committed to the lesson you are. The anger and frustration that you may be feeling because you have been asked to take particularly difficult students at a moment's notice, with no preparation, should be hidden and left for another time. Just as hostility won't help to manage the behaviour of the group, neither will a passive attitude. The desperate, passive appeal – 'Please be good for me today, come on guys, please, just for me' – won't help your management of behaviour. Your energy levels need to be high and your assertive attitude resolute. Try surprising them with your enthusiasm for the work: it can be very infectious.

In the opening minutes of the session you need to make your expectations absolutely clear and model your response to appropriate and inappropriate behaviours. Have your rules or routines written on the board or desk and make sure they are in a format the students can understand easily (words, signs, symbols, pictures, etc.). Explain very briefly that you will be using this framework and then immediately reward two or three students who have followed your instructions from the beginning. I always find it useful to have tangible and high-level rewards such as positive notes or referral to a colleague whom the students know well. This may not match the rewards structure you usually employ, but it will send a clear message to the students that making good choices in a withdrawal session is worthwhile.

Small-group withdrawal sessions

Here is an example of the rules, rewards and consequences for small-group withdrawal sessions:

Rules

1. Follow instructions the first time they are given.
2. Stay on task.
3. Work without disturbing others.

Rewards

1. Verbal praise.
2. Positive note.
3. Positive referral.

Sanctions

1. Verbal warning.
2. Moving to a place of the LSA's choice.
3. Time out.

The sanctions that you employ can also be adjusted to make it clear to students that they can expect no leniency from you. It is sensible to have a planned procedure defined for calling on support or sending the student back to the classroom.

LSAs know that the withdrawal group can be sabotaged by the quality of the work: 'We did this last week', 'Please no more word searches!', 'My group is away today and I can't work without them.', 'Sir has got our books.' Taking withdrawal groups is hard enough but when the work has been set with little thought it can be like walking through treacle on a cold day. If the work is inappropriate, you need to speak to the regular teacher as soon as possible. Explain that you found the work difficult to follow and ask for more guidance and information the next time. There is not always time to negotiate with the regular teacher before you take the group out but you need to be consistent in your feedback to them. You might write them a note at the end of the session recording those students who received rewards and sanctions (purely for information rather than action). By demonstrating your commitment you are building your relationship with the regular teacher and making them think twice before setting similar work in future. If these discussions have no impact on the quality of cover work, you will need to consider approaching their line manager or a senior member of staff. This is particularly important if you find yourself covering classes for an absent teacher or find yourself with work that merely occupies rather than extends the learner. Be prepared in case the work provided is of particularly poor quality, or there is none set. Having a back-up plan in your bag may save you. If you decide early in the session to move away from the work set, your feedback to the regular teacher needs to explain gently why you felt it was necessary.

Under no circumstances, no matter how frustrated you are, should you undermine the regular teacher in front of students. This might be as simple as displaying your displeasure at the quality of the work or rifling through the teacher's desk and complaining that there are no board pens in the drawers. The students have had more time to develop a relationship with their regular teacher, and are likely to respond defensively to any negative comments. You have a professional duty to air your frustrations in an appropriate way and at an appropriate time.

At the end of the session make a point of leaving the room tidy and organised. Have an established routine for clearing away. Finding your teaching area in a disorganised mess when it has been used by another group is very frustrating and time consuming. Judgements about your professionalism are made not simply on the quality of your teaching but also on the way in which you manage behaviour, feedback to the regular teacher and the condition in which you leave the classroom.

Reflecting on practice

Arriving for a day's supply teaching at a primary school in Newham, East London, I was shown to my classroom by the headteacher. The fact that it was a 'Portakabin' was disappointing but not surprising; but what I found inside was shocking. There were no displays, random bits of students' work were piled high on most surfaces and resources were scattered everywhere. The headteacher explained that the class had not been taught by a regular teacher since the beginning of the school year − it was now April. I remember thinking at the time, 'OK, but does that excuse the state of the classroom?' I diplomatically bit my lip.

As I cleared a space on the carpet for the class, I anticipated a raging hoard of feral children running me ragged all day. As they started to arrive I quickly changed my ideas. They were polite, welcoming, eager to learn and followed instructions. I think they were relieved to see an actual teacher in the classroom! Together we set about creating displays, organising the classroom, dusting off the reading scheme, saving and displaying work and making activity areas. Nothing revolutionary, just simple classroom organisation and presentation. By the end of the day a classroom stood out from the Portakabin. The headteacher arrived to sign my form and was taken aback. She was amazed and impressed that I had taken the time and effort to improve the learning environment and asked me to stay for the rest of the term. I was only too pleased to accept; the children were lovely and I sensed that they would appreciate the consistency.

Having reflected on this experience and been in the position of engaging supply teachers I am convinced that the expectations of them are simply too low. The headteacher expected very little from me and clearly had expected little from those who had gone before. If schools allow supply staff to turn up on the bell, leave at 3.15 and merely babysit in between, then they are shooting themselves in the foot. Good supply teachers (and there are many) know that it is not enough simply to turn up, supervise chaos and then leave. They also know that the more committed and enthusiastic they are to teaching the class the more chance they have of success. Furthermore they know how to get repeat work. Good supply teachers accept the same level of responsibility for all aspects of teaching and learning as regular staff, including general housekeeping duties.

If you arrived at your local surgery to find a locum doctor who told you that he wasn't interested in doing any work and he was getting paid at the end of the day anyway you would probably report him to the General Medical Council. So why accept a parallel lack of professionalism from a lazy supply teacher only interested in their wages?

Withdrawal session checklist

✔ Check the procedure for calling on assistance from senior colleagues.

✔ Display and enforce a seating plan.

✔ Meet students at the door with name labels.

✔ After the register, briefly introduce the rules, rewards and sanctions structure.

✔ Apply and model the rewards structure by delivering immediate rewards to 2 or 3 students.

✔ Apply and model the sanctions structure when appropriate but preferably as early as possible in the lesson.

✔ Have a group reward that everyone is working towards – a five-minute game at the end of the session, listening to music while working, etc.

✔ Record (for information only) the rewards and sanctions that you distribute in the lesson.

✔ Make a point of leaving the room tidy and orderly.

✔ Feed back to the regular teacher as positively as possible.

✔ Follow up on any incidents and referrals to senior staff.

Watch out for . . .

✔ Students trying to leave the room. Make it clear to the students that as this is a withdrawal session there will be no opportunity to leave the room (notwithstanding urgent toilet visits) without prior written permission. This will prevent students roaming the corridors and advertising to the rest of the school that they have got one over on the LSA.

✔ Passing over incidents and not following them up. You have a responsibility to follow up incidents that occur while you are in charge. Colleagues will appreciate and recognise your commitment to the students and school if you make it clear that you would like to be as involved as possible in following up incidents or rewards.

✔ Lessons with students who are much older or younger than you regularly teach. You may need to make adjustments in your physical and verbal language. Raising your voice to a Year 1 class may elicit a different response to that of Year 6 students, and give you some unpredictable results. I remember reducing an entire Year 2 class to tears by inadvertently raising my voice above their level of tolerance, after spending three weeks working with much older children.

Exercise

Create a photocopiable feedback sheet to use when you withdraw students for a colleague. Provide a strong model for your expectations of cover work and students may well reciprocate. You might like to consider including:

- An opportunity to give positive feedback on individual students.
- Space to record details of students who reach the upper levels of the sanctions list (for information rather than action).
- A checklist for the teacher to quickly and easily give feedback on the work set.
- A box to say where the work/resources have been left.

There are proformas you can create on the CD-ROM.

Key ideas summary

Key idea	Benefit for the LSA	Benefit for the students
Before the lesson read through the cover work and check procedures and routines.	Preparing for the lesson in advance gives you more time in class to focus on the students. When incidents occur you know the correct system of referral and can use it instantly.	There is continuity in teaching and students have confidence in the LSA.
Meet and greet students at the door with enthusiasm for the lesson.	Demonstrates a clear commitment to the students and the lesson. Communicates a proactive and assertive approach to management of behaviour.	Raises expectations about the level of work required in the lesson and discourages negative responses to the absence of their teacher.
As a first step explain the rules, rewards and sanctions that will operate in the session.	Creates a clear, simple and usable framework for the management of behaviour.	Students are able to predict your responses to appropriate and inappropriate behaviour. They begin to view you as fair and consistent.
Model your response to appropriate and inappropriate behaviour by using the rewards and sanctions early in the session.	Establishes your control of the class and clearly communicates your expectations.	Students understand that their behaviour has a direct effect on your response.
Leave the room tidy and organised and give some thought to feeding back to the regular teacher.	Colleagues make positive judgements about your professionalism and commitment to teaching their students.	Students understand that you respect their classroom. The choices they make about their behaviour in the cover lesson have a wider audience.

Plan it, write it, do it

Choose a strategy from this chapter to try out. Be realistic about your timescale for implementation and review. It takes at least 30 days to change a habit. Set the criteria by which you will measure the success of the strategy with precision.

Strategy	Resources	Start date	How I will monitor progress	Review date	Success criteria

There is a printable version of the Action Plan on the CD-ROM.

Chapter 16

Managing Behaviour Around the Site

*'Must of thought that I'd turn a blind eye, and take it.
You thought wrong.'*

Ms Dynamite, *Sick'n Tired*

The principle

Your responsibility for managing behaviour does not stop at the classroom door. If you observe students behaving inappropriately in the corridors/lunch queue/school drive/playground you must not ignore it for a quieter life, but address the behaviour. Your work is contributing to the work of the team of professionals seeking to ensure high standards of behaviour across the site. The proactive approach that you take to managing behaviour around the school can have a huge impact on the quality of your working life.

The practice

In the classroom the management of behaviour is complex, but at least you control the environment and the audience is limited. In the playground, corridors, dinner hall, car park, school gates or street outside, the game is very different. Now interactions with students happen with a larger and more diverse audience in an environment that you cannot control or predict. Your own behaviour is being scrutinised with more care and students can feel that you are encroaching on territory where they are used to more privacy and freedom. There are two things that you need to focus on: keeping your physical and verbal language clear and unambiguous; and knowing when to send for help, record and/or walk away.

Walking around the site you may observe more school rules being broken than you do in the classes in which you work. You cannot expect to deal with each misdemeanour personally or immediately and you will need to prioritise those that you do. The reason for this is pragmatic – if you stopped and intervened every time you saw a rule being challenged you might not make it across the playground before the end of break. Also there are those behaviours that need immediate intervention and those that can be recorded for discussion later: 'Hi, Adam. Thank you for arriving on time to the lesson. When I get time today I will need a quiet word about some of the poor choices you made in the lunch queue.'

With the students that you teach regularly you may begin to manage behaviour more efficiently and calmly but walking around the school and ending up in confrontations with students that you don't teach is all too easy. There may be no rules or graduated rewards/sanctions displayed or even agreed. The ratio of students to adults is even higher than it is in classes and students recognise this; some use it to their advantage. You want to address the behaviour of individuals who are engaging in what you see as inappropriate behaviour.

Strategy spotlight

Approaching a student you don't know well

If you are intervening with a student that you don't know or don't usually teach, it is worth finding out their name and form group before you approach them. Casually ask a student who is some distance away from the action for this information and it will be readily given. Demand it from the protagonist when you arrive on the scene and it will display your lack of knowledge and put you at an immediate disadvantage.

When you approach a student to discuss their behaviour in a public place your physical language counts. Approach with obvious physical respect and the chances of a positive start to the conversation are greatly increased. Try:

- Standing side by side rather than face to face.
- Making eye contact brief and gentle.
- Adopting a slow, casual approach.
- Keeping a respectful distance – double the personal space you might give a friend.
- Using gentle, subtle gestures – no pointy fingers!
- Non-verbal cues for drawing students away from their peers.

As there are unlikely to be rules displayed in social areas you will need to make the reason for your intervention immediately clear: e.g. 'Hello, Ryan. I need to have a quiet word with you, can we step aside so that we can talk in private? I have stopped you because you were running/smoking/levitating in the playground.'

Just as you would in the classroom you need to connect the observed behaviour with the appropriate rule. If your school relies on a 'code of conduct' for behaviour around the school, then use this and make a note to appeal to the senior management for an agreement on clear rules for social areas. Remember to use a model of the student's previous appropriate behaviour to encourage them to make better choices.

Perhaps your greatest contribution to managing behaviour around the school site is your presence. If you have your coffee in the playground, your lunch with the students and are ever-present in the corridor outside classrooms then students will see consistency in your expectations for behaviour both in and out of class. They will grow used to your interventions in social areas and your presence will slowly have an impact on their behaviour. Hide in the staffroom or take the long way round to the library to avoid potential problem areas and you risk being effective only within the confines of your teaching space.

Showing commitment to the management of behaviour around the school has a number of benefits. Once you have established yourself not simply in the classroom but around the site the 'pay-off' will be significant and positively affect each working day. When students realise that you are going to intervene (or record and chase) rather than ignore, they start to correct their behaviour before you arrive (or at least smile knowingly and wait until you have passed). Instead of walking into regular and unpleasant negative exchanges with students you take the opportunity to have positive interactions as you move around the school. Cover lessons are easier, and break and after-school duties calmer and more enjoyable. Students are more used to having you around and you are more relaxed in their company. Everybody benefits.

Supporting colleagues effectively

Unless you are a senior teacher, you are more likely to come to the aid of a colleague in social areas than in a classroom. When a colleague asks for support, be ready to listen carefully before deciding on your course of action. Judging how you can give the most effective support for a colleague who appears to need assistance but has not asked for it, is more difficult. Try simply stopping, watching and waiting. Your colleague can then decide when, how and if they want support. If the situation that you walk into is a confrontation between a student and an adult (or looks likely to develop into one) you might want to separate the two and give everyone time to calm down. 'Could you wait there, Alexandra, I want to speak to Mr Patel in private and then I will have a chance to talk to you,' not only buys you time but gives everyone the opportunity to consider their next move. While the other teacher explains the situation, control your verbal and physical reaction to the information. You are being observed carefully by the student involved to see if you are rushing to a judgement. With your face as neutral as possible listen actively to your colleague and either adjourn the decision-making for later in the day or move the discussion to a less public area: 'Thank you, yes we need to deal with this. I will take Alexandra to wait in reception/wait with her form tutor [somewhere neutral and safe, as opposed to outside the head's office] so that we can organise a better time/place to resolve this.'

If you are supporting a colleague who has lost control of the situation and/or themselves or is in the middle of a loud conversation your, 'Mr Patel, can we talk in private?' may need to be more forceful and rhetorical. Another useful way to break into the confrontation is to address the student first, picking up on their immediate behaviour rather than making any judgement on what has gone before: 'Wayne, I know you can be calmer and more polite than this,' or 'Wayne, we need to move this conversation to somewhere more private.' Your comments to the student should serve two purposes: to disengage them from the argument with your colleague; and gently suggest to everyone that there would be a better way of resolving the problem.

Fighting in social areas

It is more common for fights to break out in social areas than in lessons; in the lunch hall, playground or corridors. They are often planned so that there are few adults in the vicinity and so it is likely that you will arrive while the fight is in progress or to pick up the pieces. There may be a problem with other students crowding and, in some cases, encouraging the fighters. In these cases resist the temptation to rush to an instant judgement on blame but use the strength of your voice to instruct the crowds to leave – 'It's over, finished, *we* will deal with this now' – while treating the fighters equally but separately – 'Kylie go with Mrs Wallis, Sheena come with me.' The fall out from a fight can be exacerbated by assumptions of guilt, 'Fighting again, Darren, right you'll be going home,' or by unequal treatment of students, 'Go and clean yourself up, Shona; Eleanor, it's the head's office for you.' Instead ask witnesses to record their versions of events in isolation and take time to reach your judgements on appropriate sanctions or referrals. Many schools have found the use of CCTV in social areas has reduced incidents of violence and made it much more straightforward to apportion blame after the event.

Fights at the school gates

Nobody relishes duty at the school gates at the end of the day. In some schools the gates attract unwelcome visitors: excluded students, dealers, students from rival schools, older teenagers in cars, etc. LSAs are rightly unsure of their jurisdiction on the street outside and managing physical confrontation is more complex and more dangerous. If you are supervising at the school gates you should not do so alone and to reduce risk further you ought to have a walkie-talkie to call for more support. If a fight breaks out in the street outside the school, call for more support immediately and ask students who are leaving the site to return to the reception area and wait for instructions. If you see weapons being used or produced, call the police, protect those in immediate danger and record what you see. In most of the schools I have worked in where such fights are commonplace, the police are already nearby or waiting outside the gates to assist the safe passage of students.

Watch out for . . .

✔ Audiences gathering – deal with them as soon as possible as they will inevitably become involved and are never going to improve the situation.

✔ Judging situations too quickly or too harshly – beware of heightened emotional states and that you may only be seeing an unrepresentative snapshot of the incident.

✔ Shouting empty threats from a distance and walking away without engaging with the student: 'I can see you, I am going to report you to the head.'

✔ Jumping into confrontation too quickly – take your time, control the interaction at your own pace.

Reflecting on practice

Extreme break duty

Break or playground duty was never a convenient or particularly welcome duty. I would often find myself caught up with dealing with the aftermath of a busy Year 9 lesson only to be harried outside by the PE teacher who was a stickler for 'duties'. It was not that I thought it unimportant, only that those immediate crises inevitably overtake you. Ryan was not going to thank me for leaving him in tears, bag broken, with baying hordes waiting for him, so that I could see to the masses outside. In a school of 1400 the playground is a very busy place.

That day I had arrived on time. I had thrown caution to the wind in not preparing the room properly for the arrival of Year 11, set 4 after break (I knew that I would regret it later) and with the voice of the PE teacher ringing in my ears ventured out into the cold. In my previous schools, playground duty had always been a fairly calm affair: dissuading the smokers by patrolling their haunts, cuts and bruises, a bit of pushing and shoving but nothing that I found particularly dangerous or threatening. That day the atmosphere in the playground was very different.

Two distinct groups existed in the school and in the community. They learnt together in some harmony, considering their turbulent history. But there had been trouble outside school between the adults in the community and the two groups of boys lined up at opposite ends of the playground preparing to settle the score. As I watched they slowly moved towards each other as colleagues ran for assistance. I found myself in the middle of the encroaching armies and decided to stay put. I adjusted my body language so that I was not threatening anyone and in order not to show preference to either group stood facing away from both, looking down. Now I am not a small man, but there were individuals bigger than me and regardless of my size there were upwards of 200 students involved. They stopped either side of me and I calmly explained, briefly looking at each lead boy in turn, that it wasn't going to happen here, now, with me in the middle of it. They paused, thought and with a general mummer of agreement walked away.

The senior management team watching the whole encounter on CCTV breathed a heavy sigh of relief, whilst making a mental note to have stern words with me about my personal safety.

Now I am not claiming to have solved the conflict, nor am suggesting you jump into the middle of gang fights on a whim, but this serves as an example of how simple verbal and physical language can help to calm even the most extreme situations around the school.

Exercise

List five behaviours that are a common annoyance while walking around the school:

1 ....

2 ....

3 ....

4 ....

5 ....

Now prioritise and code these behaviours using the following categories:

Record and challenge later	RC
Call for urgent support	CS
Wait for support to arrive	WS
Verbally intervene	Vi
Physically intervene	Pi

Behaviours	Response
1.	....
2.	....
3.	....
4.	....
5.	....

Graffiti

Minor rule breaks

Aggressive behaviour towards staff

Smoking

Verbal bullying

Swearing

Fighting

Racist language

Threats to other students

Breaking school property

Out of class without permission

Running in corridors

Incorrect uniform

Suspicion of drink/drugs

Key ideas summary

Key idea	Benefit for the LSA	Benefit for the students
Do not ignore or avoid inappropriate behaviour around the school.	LSAs assert their right to monitor and manage behaviour in all areas of the school.	Students know that their inappropriate behaviour will be challenged and result in consequences.
Keep your physical and verbal language clear and simple.	Confrontations are discouraged, communication clear and unassailable. Defensive reactions from students are minimised.	Students recognise the challenge to their behaviour and do not feel personally threatened.
Plan and structure your intervention with care.	The adult controls when the intervention starts and ends.	Students are given clear instructions and/or choices.
When supporting colleagues, be quick to listen and slow to judge.	The LSA avoids being drawn into a confrontation or undermining colleagues.	Students in a heightened emotional state know that they are going to have the opportunity to speak and be listened to.

Plan it, write it, do it

Choose a strategy from this chapter to try out. Be realistic about your timescale for implementation and review. It takes at least 30 days to change a habit. Set the criteria by which you will measure the success of the strategy with precision.

Strategy	Resources	Start date	How I will monitor progress	Review date	Success criteria

There is a printable version of the Action Plan on the CD-ROM.

Chapter 17

Working in Schools in Special Measures and Extreme Circumstances

'I won't say ours was a tough school, but we had our own coroner. We used to write essays like: "What I'm going to be IF I grow up."'

Lenny Bruce

The principle

The behaviour of students is a key determinant when OFSTED decides that a school has 'serious weaknesses' or must be placed in Special Measures. The institutional change that is demanded is accelerated and unforgiving; it has positive and negative outcomes for everyone. Even in a school in the most desperate circumstances you can successfully manage and improve the behaviour of students you are working alongside.

The practice

You are working extremely hard and often with some success in a very challenging school. The school has failed OFSTED and HMI (Her Majesty's Inspectors) have just announced the school is being placed in Special Measures or some lesser label requiring radical change. You now have the additional pressures of intensive inspection and overhaul of policy and practice sitting uncomfortably alongside individuals and groups who need a great deal of skilled behaviour management.

When your school is placed in Special Measures or identified as having 'serious weaknesses' your responsibilities, accountability and workload increase. You now have to satisfy the urgent demands of frequent inspections, nervous senior managers, stressed class teachers, concerned parents and confused students. Time that you previously guarded as your own will be trampled on, your home covered in action plans, new procedures, minutes of meetings, new policy documents, etc., and your social/family life becomes a distant memory. You will be tired, probably ill and at times when you need to be most effective, continually distracted by competing agendas. Tempers are frayed and verbal and physical confrontations between students and adults can become more commonplace. In addition, while staff have retreat to the safety of the staffroom (or dark cupboard!) to catch up on paperwork, the behaviour of students in the corridors begins to deteriorate. Whatever your role your workload will increase significantly.

The external pressures on your work and students can and will compound existing difficulties with challenging behaviour. While you are left to deal with the disruptive behaviour of students outside the classroom door, as well as inside it, you notice some colleagues desperately looking through the job ads. You may be rightly apprehensive of what is about to come.

Even though the staffroom may be in turmoil, the local press camped out on the school drive and parents trying to move their children to a different school, your primary focus should still be the management of your groups/individuals. As you are led through meetings explaining new inspection arrangements prioritise your time carefully. Don't allow your personal time management to be trampled by new deadlines and the demands of paperwork. Some of these new demands can be renegotiated, some fed gradually. Amidst all of these new hoops that you are busy trying to jump through or avoid, there are still classes to be managed and students to be cushioned from the inspection fallout. Even the most experienced LSAs can be shaken. Protect your time, protect your students and protect yourself. When push comes to shove it is your work in class that really matters to everyone, including even the most rigorous inspectors.

Negative publicity, low morale, loss of parental confidence and damage to the school's reputation can have a damaging effect on students as well as the confidence and self-esteem of the staff. Schools that are keen to this danger make sure that the students are kept well informed of events. By sharing the problems and in straightforward language explaining what is going to be done, a collegiate responsibility is defined.

In the classroom you will need to be prepared to challenge misconceptions, 'Why is this school no good? Are we all stupid?' and calm fears, 'Are they going to close the school?', 'Are you going to get sacked, Sir?' With the school in a period of change and instability it is important that you are utterly consistent in your management of behaviour. Reinforce the learning rituals, resist changes in rules, rewards and sanctions, and keep your levels of acknowledgement and praise high. Reassure the students that regardless of what is happening outside the classroom they are still capable of achieving great things, of proving the doubters wrong, of surprising even the most enthusiastic critics. Schools can, and do, change radically for the better. Even those in the most extreme circumstances can be turned around.

Unfortunately there are many casualties in the fallout from heavy inspection: senior management are a common target. Many colleagues, who in a different school might be successful and highly valued, can be moved aside, retired early or moved out of positions of responsibility. Others work themselves ragged to take the school out of the spotlight only to move jobs as soon as possible afterwards to recover, and many leave the profession exhausted and disillusioned after long periods of intensive inspection. Much depends on the influence of the senior management team over the pace of change. The quality of the inspection team is also a key determinant. Whilst there are undoubtedly many sensitive and diplomatic inspectors there are also some who wield their power with too much enjoyment and without empathy for individuals. It is the latter group who do most damage. 'Hands up who wants to be an inspector'? may be the best way to identify those who ought not to be in the profession.

> ### Working as a team
>
> Keeping a clear focus on your own teaching does not preclude working as part of a staff team to improve behaviour. In all schools, and particularly in those with significant behaviour issues, there will be a small number of key staff who have a major influence on students. Align yourself with one of these key members of staff. This might a formal arrangement where you seek regular support and advice, or more likely an informal one, where you ask them to pass by or visit at critical times. Students will recognise the alliances that staff form and may adjust their decisions on behaviour accordingly. That is why the supply teacher who has no regular team within the school is often identified by students as an easy target. The newly qualified teacher who is mentored by the deputy headteacher is a more risky proposition for students choosing to disrupt.

Changing an atmosphere

Schools where the corridors and social areas have become almost no-go areas for teachers have found that the staff working en masse can have a direct and immediate impact. One or two adults patrolling the grounds at break or monitoring corridors can have little calming effect on the atmosphere; it is just firefighting. However, when larger numbers of staff:

- patrol the grounds,
- stand outside classrooms at the changeover of lessons,
- help out at the school gates before and after school,
- sign up to a strategic plan for enforcing no-go areas,
- minimise permission for students to be out of classrooms,
- rigidly enforce and use 'out of lessons' passes,
- swiftly respond to a request to assist a colleague,

there is an immediate impact on student behaviour. Of course there needs to be a willingness to confront poor behaviour, but with the staff out in numbers there is less chance of confrontation exploding and more chance of support arriving if or when it does. There is obviously an issue with disruption of allocated morning and lunch breaks but the outcome is worth the sacrifice and inconvenience. Instead of the corridors being full of wall climbers, crowd surfers and crisp sprinklers, with collaboration between staff they can be calmer areas allowing smaller children to walk with more confidence.

Watch out for . . .

✔ Deadlines that are imposed on an unrealistic timescale. Be prepared to protect your own time and time set aside for tasks that are directly related to effective teaching and behaviour management.

✔ Volunteering for too much, too soon. There may be some exciting 'professional development opportunities' that you wish you hadn't saddled yourself with later in the term.

✔ Taking too much time over tasks that are purely administrative. Set clear limits on the amount of time you will give to tasks that are unrelated to effective teaching and learning.

✔ Having your enthusiasm sapped by colleagues who have given up on their students, the school and themselves. Stay away from the doubters or they will drag you into their pit of despair.

✔ Colleagues who are struggling – give time to help others, you may need their support tomorrow.

Reflecting on practice

'No trainers means no trainers' – enforcing a rule

The strongest team and the one that can have most impact is the whole staff team. When staff in extreme circumstances have unity of purpose and keep to agreed procedures they can effect significant change

Students would wear trainers to school as a matter of course at Park Community School. It was by no means the worst rule break in the school but enforcing it was a key step in restoring the balance of power in an increasingly tense environment. The original rule of 'black or brown formal shoes' had been worn down over many years. This was partly because students were so persistent in their desire to wear trainers, partly because teachers had grown tired of confronting students and partly because parents, trying to keep up with the price of trainers, did not have enough money to buy two pairs of shoes. Mobilising the whole staff into pushing the rule break to the top of their radar, using a rigid procedure supported at all levels of management, and communicating clearly with parents solved the problem. All parents were written to and given notice that the rule would be strictly applied after the summer break. The procedure for students with trainers was simple. Parents would be contacted, students would be sent home to change and as a last resort they would be kept out of lessons until school shoes appeared. Only a medical note would excuse a student in trainers and these would need to be black ones.

As a staff body we would confront any student wearing trainers and extra checks were put in place at key points – leaving PE/Drama, leaving the last lesson of the day, end of morning and lunch breaks. At the start of the new term there were 50 students who arrived in trainers, a week later it was 28 and within a month there were no students out of school uniform. A great deal of work had been put in by all concerned. Nobody looked forward to those difficult conversations with parents ('Yes, but I can't afford to buy him another pair of shoes'), or to isolating students from their classes, but the effect was indisputable. The process and the product served to prove a much-needed point for the staff: it was possible to effect significant change in student behaviour. We then began looking for other things that we wanted to change . . .

Exercise

Effective time management will allow you to allocate sufficient time to plan, design and implement behaviour management strategies and structures. There may well be issues that may have arisen since the school was given its new label that need time planning. As the school moves into a period of change and your workload increases effective time management will keep you sane. Managing your time has positive benefits on your emotional control. Tired, stressed and irritable LSAs who are being ground down by work are not going to be able to give their best work in the classroom.

Go through the strategies checklist below ticking off those that you already use and selecting three ideas to adopt immediately and three to introduce over the next few weeks:

Strategies to help you manage your time effectively

	Already use	Adopt now	Use soon
Prioritise tasks on a written list – decide which tasks are urgent, which are important and those that are unimportant.	❑	❑	❑
Close your door when you are working alone.	❑	❑	❑
Make appointments with yourself – set aside blocks of time for important work, planning and free time.	❑	❑	❑
Ask for timed agendas for all meetings.	❑	❑	❑
Reduce paperwork – keep memos short, handle each piece of paper only once.	❑	❑	❑
Determine your most productive time and use it carefully.	❑	❑	❑
Set times when you are available to answer questions and provide help for others.	❑	❑	❑
Schedule your work.	❑	❑	❑
Schedule rewards at the end of heavy periods of work.	❑	❑	❑
If you can't find a quiet office or space, post a sign to indicate you don't want to be disturbed.	❑	❑	❑
Establish times when you will answer or return phone calls.	❑	❑	❑
Establish times when you read and respond to emails.	❑	❑	❑
Communicate with colleagues/students the times when you are available.	❑	❑	❑
Schedule weekly reviews of progress.	❑	❑	❑

	Already use	Adopt now	Use soon
Make use of little bursts of time to achieve one or two longer tasks.	❑	❑	❑
Be realistic about the amount of time you will give each task – 15 minutes per report, 30 minutes responding to memos, etc.	❑	❑	❑
When immediate demands are placed on your time be prepared to renegotiate them.	❑	❑	❑
Use 'to do' lists with clear deadlines.	❑	❑	❑
Use a Dictaphone or voice recorder on your phone to record incidents that will need writing up.	❑	❑	❑

Know where your time goes by creating a time log to monitor and improve your efficiency. Use it to bounce back requests for immediate calls on your time. Use the spreadsheet on the CD-ROM to record use of your time over the course of a week.

Key ideas summary

Key idea	Benefit for the LSA	Benefit for the students
Hold your classroom teaching and management of behaviour as your primary focus.	You have a clear priority for your time management. You will be judged on your class teaching.	The standard of teaching is maintained and responses to behaviour remain consistent.
Be prepared to challenge negative reflections and misconceptions from your students.	Your high expectations are not undermined by rumour and misinformation.	Students have an opportunity to ask questions and understand how the changes will affect them.
Reinforce and develop supportive relationships with key colleagues.	You can seek advice and support working as part of a team.	Students see adults working together and modelling team-work.
Be proactive in managing behaviour outside the room you are working in. Work with neighbouring colleagues to keep movement between lessons calm.	Students entrance to the classroom is calmer and there is less noise from the corridors invading your lessons. The support of colleagues makes confrontation less likely.	Students feel safer walking to and from lessons; they know that the rules apply in the corridors.

Plan it, write it, do it

Choose a strategy from this chapter to try out. Be realistic about your timescale for implementation and review. It takes at least 30 days to change a habit. Set the criteria by which you will measure the success of the strategy with precision.

Strategy	Resources	Start date	How I will monitor progress	Review date	Success criteria

There is a printable version of the Action Plan on the CD-ROM.

 # Afterword

'Outside ideas of right doing and wrong doing there is a field.
I'll meet you there.'
Mevlana Celaleddin Rumi, philosopher and mystic of Islam

Behaviour in schools and colleges has never been a bigger nationwide issue. The public debate rages. Influential popularist media feed the demand for information by naming, shaming and attacking vulnerable children and schools. Politicians who couldn't manage the average Year 3 class try to convince everyone that they have the solution. Parents feel under attack as they are blamed for everything that doesn't stick to those who work in schools. While everyone searches for the magic bullet, children listen to the debate and wonder if the adult world has lost control.

The issue is not going to go away on its own, but teachers and LSAs are in a unique position to effect change. There are many who have excellent skills in managing behaviour using strategies that they have tailored for their students. There are strategies that work, people who know how to apply and adapt them and teachers who want to learn. The key issue is not whether we know what works; the issue is training.

Behaviour management training for LSAs is at worst patchy and at best infrequent. When people outside of education hear that training in behaviour management on initial training courses has such a low priority they are shocked (LSAs know this already to their cost). Managing behaviour is a core teaching skill, yet most adults in the classroom are lucky if they have had one INSET day to learn more about it, let alone received ongoing training. Whilst the single training day can have a positive impact, it is rarely an effective standalone.

LSAs need training that they can access throughout their careers; intensive initial training followed by regular opportunities to revisit, rework and remember techniques. We *need* to: include competencies in behaviour management as part of assessing effective teaching; introduce them in self-reviews, observations and departmental training, and share good practical tips between schools on managing behaviour. As ever in education it is partly a question of resources and partly willingness of staff.

The choice is clear. We can wait for society to re-establish the authority of educators or we can go and re-establish it ourselves.

Bibliography

Barker, C. (1977) *Theatre Games*, London: Methuen.

Biddulph, S. (2003) *Why boys are different – and how to help them become happy and well-ballanced men*, London: Thorsons.

Britton J. (1970) *Language and Learning*, London: Penguin Books.

Canter, L. (1992) *Assertive Discipline*, Santa Monica CA: Lee Canter and Associates.

DfES (2002) *Guidance on the use of restrictive physical interventions for staff working with children and adults 2002*, The Stationery Office.

DfES (2004) *Safeguarding Children in Education*, DfES 00272004, The Stationery Office.

DfES (2004) *Every Child Matters: Change for Children in Schools*, The Stationery Office.

DfES (2005) *The Report of the Practitioner Group on School Behaviour and Discipline (The Steer Report)*, The Stationery Office.

Goleman, D. (1995) *Emotional Intelligence*, New York: Bantam Books.

Gardner, H. (1983) *Frames of Mind*, New York: Basic Books.

Lewicki, R. J and Edwards, C Tomlinson, 'Trust and Trust Building' *Beyond Intractibility*, eds Guy Burgess and Heidi Burgess, Conflict Research Consortium, University of Colorado, Boulder.

Mahony, T. (2003) *Words Work*, Carmarthen, Wales: Crown House Publishing.

OFSTED (2005) *Managing Challenging Behaviour*, The Stationery Office.

Rogers, B. (1991) *You Know the Fair Rule*, Harlow: Pearson Education.

Sigamn, A. (2005) *Remotely Controlled*, New York: Random House.

Vygotsky, L. (1986 rev. edition) *Thought and Language*, Massachusetts: MIT Press.

Index

Licensing Agreement

This book comes with a CD. By opening this package you are agreeing to be bound by the following:

The files are copyright Pearson Education. **THIS CD IS PROVIDED FREE OF CHARGE, AS IS, AND WITHOUT WARRANTY OF ANY KIND, EITHER EXPRESSED OR IMPLIED, INCLUDING, BUT NOT LIMITED TO, THE IMPLIED WARRANTIES OF MERCHANTABILITY AND FITNESS FOR A PARTICULAR PURPOSE.** Neither the book publisher nor its dealers and distributors assumes any liability for any alleged or actual damages arising from use of this CD.